the RAVEN'S RETURN

the RAVEN'S RETURN

The Influence of Psychological Trauma on Individuals and Culture

EMMETT EARLY

Chiron Publications ❖ Wilmette, Illinois

Library of Congress Catalog Card Number: 93–22345

Printed in the United States of America.

Editing and book design by Siobhan Drummond.
Cover design by Julie Burleigh.

Library of Congress Cataloging-in-Publication Data:

Early, Emmett.
The raven's return : the influence of psychological trauma on individuals and culture / Emmett Early.
p. cm.
Includes bibliographical references and index.
ISBN 0–933029–70–5 : $14.95
1. Post-traumatic stress disorder. 2. Psychic trauma. 3. Archetype (Psychology) in literature. I. Title.
RC552.P67E25 1993
616.85'21—dc20 93–22345
CIP

ISBN 0–933029–70–5

Dedicated with love to

Ann Early,

Liam Early,

and

Judy Early

Contents

Introduction

"I couldn't bear to think about it; and yet, somehow, I couldn't think about nothing else."
Mark Twain, *The Adventures of Huckleberry Finn*

As a survivor of childhood psychological trauma, I didn't have it as bad as Huckleberry Finn, but I certainly identified with him. My mother had died when I was a child, and I was raised by an alcoholic father. However, my father worked steadily all his adult life, and it was he who first read aloud to me about Huckleberry Finn. Huck's father beat him, imprisoned him, and stole from him, and Huck's trek down the Mississippi with Jim can be viewed as an odyssey of escape and recovery from psychological trauma.

The loss of my mother when I was seven is the most significant single event in my life. There were certainly other events that were momentous to me, in which it seemed that I had stepped into Huck's archetypal river, but with each of those subsequent events I had to refer back to the loss of my mother. Her death set the template upon which my life has been patterned.

In 1965, when I was in a period of transition in my life, I came upon C. G. Jung's *The Psychology of the Unconscious* (later republished as volume five in the *Collected Works*) in the San Francisco Public Library. It seemed then that the floodgates opened in my unconscious and dreams poured forth. It was then that I began analysis, and it was Jung's influence that got me into psychology as a profession. Later, in 1979, when I was asked to open a Veterans Administration outreach center for Vietnam veterans in Seattle, Washington, I found that I had stepped into another archetypal river. This was a collective river of a traumatic historical event that was a maelstrom of emotion from shadowy war trauma survivors. It was my first *conscious* experience of being swept up into an archetype. I invite those who scoff at Jung's concept of the archetypal experience to examine closely the repeating experience of the survivor of psychological trauma in general, and particularly the experience of the combat veteran.

My clinical training, as good as it was, had not given me a good understanding of the problems of psychological trauma. Jung had written very little that directly dealt with trauma ("The Therapeutic Value of Abreaction" (Jung 1928) being the chief exception), but I felt that his theory of complexes and his understanding of shadow and of unconscious contamination had prepared me to work with war veterans. At that time, in 1979, there was very little written in general about psychological trauma. The works of Kardiner (1941), Lifton, Niederland, and Krystal, all of whom contributed to Krystal's seminal study of Nazi concentration camp survivors (Krystal 1967), along with Jung, were my resources. Primarily it was my personal experience with psychological trauma, the death of my mother in my childhood, that I drew upon to relate to war survivors. The rejection that the Vietnam veterans experienced as society's shadow I knew intuitively I had experienced as an emotionally neglected motherless child.

When my mother died in the late forties, my family was living in a black ghetto that had been created as housing for shipyard workers (Marin City, California). A black woman took over as a visiting caregiver. For the rest of my life, I will associate the outsider's status to my mother's death. Later, as a young teenager in the first days of rock and roll, I scorned the popular music. I was an aficionado of rhythm and blues and a petty hood loitering in the pool hall in downtown San Rafael. In the late fifties, I was attracted to bebop jazz and the beatniks, with their imagery as the society's shadows, the children of Saturn, if you will.

I will describe in chapter two, "Unwanted Consciousness," how Jung's psychology prepared me to deal with the countertransference of posttraumatic stress disorder (PTSD). Jung understood the trauma complex, but I knew psychological trauma. I knew that what I was experiencing at the Vets Center was the product of unconscious energy and the canalizing of libido. Later, in 1981, after I left the Veterans Administration for private practice, I wrote about my reaction as a way to release the emotional pressure of the experience. In an essay I called "The Quick and the Dead, Junior," I described some the images that were constellated by my work.

"The Quick and the Dead, Junior"

Energy was the most remarkable thing about the Vets Center. Energy from my staff, energy from the clients, energy everywhere but from the moribund Veterans Administration. My first image was that of Ben Hur on a chariot pulled by a team of wild horses. "Ain't no use saying `Whoa!' Doc. They can't hear you anyway." My staff counselors were hired especially for the job and were combat vets themselves. "The quick and the dead, Junior," one of the counselors would chant, pacing the floor, fists clenched, like a gladiator waiting to be released: "The quick and the dead."

When I interviewed applicants for my staff, the second fellow I talked with was a deadly serious Hispanic ex-marine. He told me a recurring combat nightmare that reminded me of Picasso's *Guernica*: bulls slaughtered in Mithraic ritual. I felt drawn back to some earlier era when Christianity vied with Mithraism. Mithra, the lion-headed god, was the carrier of ancient myths and a favorite of the Roman legions because he valued courage over charity, strength over gentleness, and exalted military virtues above all others—and he especially loved *action*.

Vets began telling me their dreams and their experiences in Vietnam. The experiences still haunted them and crept into their awareness at the damndest times. "Whenever I make love, I see corpses," said one. "Images that yet fresh images beget," wrote Yeats. I thought of rapacious Saturn eating his children, blood dripping from his face like a child eating beets. I would see them all: the snipers, grunts, airborne, LRRPS (pronounced "lurps," an acronym for long-range recon patrol), medics, corpsmen, nurses, door-gunners, dog handlers, pilots, ammo handlers, corpse handlers, men who loaded chemical bombs, artillery sergeants, truck drivers, seabees, radio operators, combat engineers. . . . Soon *my* eyes became haunted, like those in the movie poster on the Vets Center wall of Werner Herzog's Aguirre, Wrath of God, the gaunt warrior who holds his slain lady in his arms, himself armored and defenseless on a jungle river raft. It was the poster that confronted the men as they ran into the bathroom to retch out the undigested odious memory of bloated corpses.

I thought of the knight in Bergman's *The Seventh Seal,* also gaunt, dolorous, returned from the Crusades, disillusioned, ideals betrayed, returned to his plague-ridden land, stalked by death. Grim. Grim. But in that movie the knight was lethargic, all his energy in the form of his lusty servant. My vets told of unrelenting death, as in Kurt Jooss's ballet dance, *The Green Table,* stomping and pounding and strutting with thunderous rapacity. Jooss choreographed the dance in Germany after the First World War. There death had an almost mechanical virility as he marched on incessantly, while about him scampered politicians like evil, gesticulating monkeys imitating men.

I talked with the warrior-survivor alienated from his land, his memory far livelier than his present life, who sits under some bush in his yard, late at night, watching his house. Like Faulkner's Colonel Sartoris returned from a defeated Confederate army, feeling undefeated, to find his land infested with Snopeses, those amoral, pernicious draft-dodgers. And remember Odysseus's rage when he returned . . . but somehow to say that Odysseus was a victim of PTSD misses the point, doesn't it?

The combat soldier in Vietnam watched dragons at night spitting fire in a stream from the sky. Cobras swooped over the forests that decayed before his eyes. His best friend jumped from his tank and had his legs blown off by a mine . . . but why don't you forget that Vietnam, Junior, and help your dad with his store?

He can shit in a rice paddy and watch the turd float away and then fly home the next day, wondering what does he say to the girls when they ask. But nobody asks who listens, and ten years later the memory sits like an RPG round lodged in his brain.

The boy watched the war on TV before going over and then the vet watched disbelievingly after he returned. "Junior, you didn't do *that,* did you?"

At night, at home, I pace the floor, fists rigid, infused with anger. "Since you've been working with the vets, you've become manic depressive," says my wife. "It ain't nothin' but a feelin', Doc," says my colleague at the Vets Center as he sticks a cigarette in his ear and lights his nose on fire.

The telephone rings: "My husband just built a bunker in the bedroom. I told him he's crazy and he told me to shut up and get down."

My client sits with his back to the wall, chair between his legs and tells me about his buddy the VC captured. They cut off his balls and stuffed them in his mouth. They found his LRRP team like that, five of them, hanging in a tree like some Dionysian precursor of Christmas. My client dreams about himself hanging there. He feels that he should have gone with them that day. He feels that he should have died in Vietnam.

Just then, amidst our tears, my boss calls from the VA and tells me my reports are late. "Psychologists are cheap," he reminds me. "I hired you because you're warm."

Late at night I walk through the bushes to my house, dog chain in my hand, warily watching the shadows for movement. I'm thinking I'd better leave these archetypes alone. My mid-brain is getting overstimulated.

Tonto, Mr. Hyde, and the Green Knight

After my stint at the Vets Center, I entered private practice with the preoccupation of better understanding psychological trauma. I began writing essays to create guideposts, herms along an unknown path. It seemed to me that psychological trauma created a disturbance that set off and illustrated the dynamics of the psyche. And it seemed, too, that trauma permeated American culture. I began giving workshops and used the literary and popular images to illustrate the trauma survivor's predicament. (When I use the word *trauma*, I mean psychological or psychic trauma.) These were the images that were stimulated in my mind at the Vets Center, and they were the images of my culture. I procured a radio tape of the first Lone Ranger episode, complete with Wheaties commercial. (When I played the tape for my workshop class at a state psychology meeting, all the old-timers smiled and entered an altered state of consciousness.) I reread classics with a new perspective: the *Odyssey*, the *Aeneid*, *Sir Gawain and the Green Knight*, and *The Strange Case of Dr. Jekyll and Mr. Hyde* described situations that beautifully illustrated the problems of the trauma survivor.

The situations I describe in these classics, and the fairy tales that I draw upon, are not to be thought of as attempts to make interpretations of the works in question, but rather as an attempt to show how the works illustrate trauma problems. I don't know why "The Adventures of the Lone Ranger" so aptly describes symbolically the dynamics of the survivor syndrome, except that it was a naive collective effort and, as such, a folk tale in modern form, much like the genesis of Homeric epics and the European fairy tales "Cinderella" and "Snow White." I think I know why Robert Louis Stevenson wrote *The Strange Case of Dr. Jekyll and Mr. Hyde*, and I'm sure it was not meant to illustrate the problems of trauma. The genesis of Sir Gawain is lost forever in my Celtic past, when the lopping of heads was the custom. I have found, however, that the recitation of these epics and tales to a contemporary audience is effective as an illustration of the problems created by a traumatic near-death experience; and to this extent the "perilous bed" of Gawain, which I describe in chapter 4, personifies the truths of anima angst, sleep disturbance, and the compulsion to repeat psychological trauma.

It is not news these days that Batman and Superman are trauma survivors bent on revenge, and that Wonder Woman spins as a way of transforming herself in a fashion not much different from that of her mythic ancestors. Once one begins to understand the symptoms of psychological trauma as they are played out in individual behavior, as opposed to the cut-and-dried nosology of PTSD, one sees the symptoms everywhere in culture.

The Raven Woodcuts

I began wood carving as a hobby shortly after I moved to Seattle. Native mythology in the Pacific Northwest is illustrated richly and abundantly. Some people hate it, but I love it. I was caught up in it on my first vacation in the San Juan Islands. The images of Raven, Dogfish, Killer Whale, and Bear are, to me, raw ancient psychic faces. As I was working with the war veterans, I began a series of wood-block carvings in which Raven was depicted as trickster and sun hero. C. G. Jung is really the inspiration for this sort of processing. My personal image of Jung is the stone carver, the artist and individualist who explores his own unconscious while keeping his feet pragmatically on the ground. I have tried on several occasions to approach Jung through the organized group discussion process, but always I feel alienated. I criticize myself for feeling that my relationship with Jung is so precious, but fortunately I had an analyst at the time, William Willeford, who assured me that the unique path was the way to go. The process of carving, the hours spent sitting on my back steps under the grey sky, listening to the crows, feeling connected to my self and the land, feeling that the Northwest Indian culture was influenced by the same climate and atmosphere, feeling that it was right for me because my ancestry, the West Coast Irish, lived in the same way, and that what I was carving was my Raven, too, the Celtic Raven of War; and that when the horror stories of the Vets Center stopped on Friday, Raven took them, ate them, and made sense of them. When my first child was born I named him Red Raven (later Liam Michael), and I carved a Raven woodblock as a birth announcement.

Different Traumas

The first chapter in this book takes the contemporary psychological understanding of PTSD and relates it to Jung's psychodynamic theory. It has always seemed to me that, while psychological trauma disorder is symptomatically the same in the abstract for all kinds of traumata, it is qualitatively different as the traumatic circumstances are different, and quantitatively different as the intensity is different. Only Jung, in his concept of the complex, really encompasses theoretically this variation of the range of psychological trauma. Reexperiencing, excitatory, and avoidance symptoms of PTSD are understandable only insofar as we understand the unique ways they are played out in human behavior. Trauma at infancy, before the development of the hippocampus, is not qualitatively the same as adult-onset trauma, yet the child who cuts on herself in her bedroom is manifesting the same basic symptom as the war survivor who compulsively gambles.

Cultural Heritage

When one is struck by a traumatic experience, the psyche that is wounded responds with the imagery of the individual's history and culture. As an Irish-American living in Seattle, I am influenced by the traditions of Western civilization, the pop culture of my childhood, and the spirits of the land that I occupy. As one African-American man said, going off to Vietnam: "Like Knights of the Round Table. We be immortal. No one can kill us" (Terry 1984, p. 38). The imagery that is called up in us and in our clients as a result of trauma is the stuff to be utilized in the processing and containment of the traumatic disruption. It is that imagery that will rejoin the survivor to the culture. It would be futile to give a man of Chinese heritage who was raised in Saigon the foreign images of Gawain or Odysseus (unless he was educated in French schools), yet there is in his heritage the archetypal image of the suffering god of healing (the wandering Buddha) which parallels Dionysus/Aesculapius/Christ. Certainly the girl who is raised in Cuba can identify with the archetypal image of the suffering goddess as Virgin Mary/Demeter/Persephone. If one can identify the imagery produced by the trauma, one is benefited and aided in the process of healing.

The next four essays deal with gender issues and trauma. To illustrate these I turn to the fairy tales of traumatized girls, "Little Red Riding Hood," "Blue Beard," "Donkey Skin," "Allerleirauh," "The Beauty and the Beast," "Cinderella," and "Snow White." When the trauma in question is the result of a natural disaster or an auto accident, it may be that gender is superfluous (there are male Cinderellas, and "Bearskin" and "Donkey Skin" are quite similar), although I am inclined to believe that the way symptoms are acted upon produces gender-specific, culturally influenced directions. The male is redeemed by the youngest daughter while the female is saved by the prince, and certainly gender specificity of trauma symptoms is pertinent and crucial when the trauma is sexual in nature.

I am influenced by Jung's concept of the contrasexual psychic image. Male and female stories are frequently mirror images. The hero's quest is pertinent to the female who is engaged in an heroic quest. There are dragons in the office of the dean or the CEO who guard the treasure hard to attain. The problems of psychic numbing, psychoactive chemical abuse, and the attainment of emotional empathy are the challenges of the survivor regardless of sex. Where the life-styles are traditional, the imagery that the psyche produces will be traditional. If the survivor is living a unique life, one that is breaking the bounds of traditional styles, then the imagery will be unique. To place the client or ourselves in a Procrustean bed, limiting ourselves to theoretical confines created by gender or race, is going to limit our possibilities for outcome. When we face the problems created by psychological trauma, we need all the help and freedom that is available. What is crucial is that, in treatment, we stick close to the client and do not impose our images as therapists onto the client, and do not allow the therapist's images to be imposed on us *a priori* if we are clients.

It is essential that the symbols we use in our process be natural and come to us spontaneously. In working with the war veterans, never having myself gone to war, I had of course to read the works at hand, but more important, I had to immerse myself in the culture of the war veterans. I had to let myself be touched and influenced by them. Many of my professional colleagues remained isolated from the survivor by institutional and intellectual insulation. However, as an outsider, I felt closer to the survivor than to the professional. As a child in Marin City, I had been a redheaded, Irish-American, fair-skinned kid of seven, alone in school in a class of African Americans. I had been recently traumatized, isolated and abandoned by the death of my mother. At age forty, I found myself alone again, after a fashion, as a white collar psychologist with a blue collar mind, a veteran who had never gone to war, surrounded by combat veterans who didn't trust me, who even actively disliked me—and I remembered my childhood, and the memory connected me.

When I was in basic training in the air force in 1959, I had a drill sergeant who liked to sing "Bye Bye Blackbird" as a marching song for drill. He liked to march us in funeral cadence and sing.

> No one here can love and understand me
> Oh what hard luck stories they all hand me
> Make my bed and light the light
> I'll arrive late tonight
> Blackbird Bye Bye.

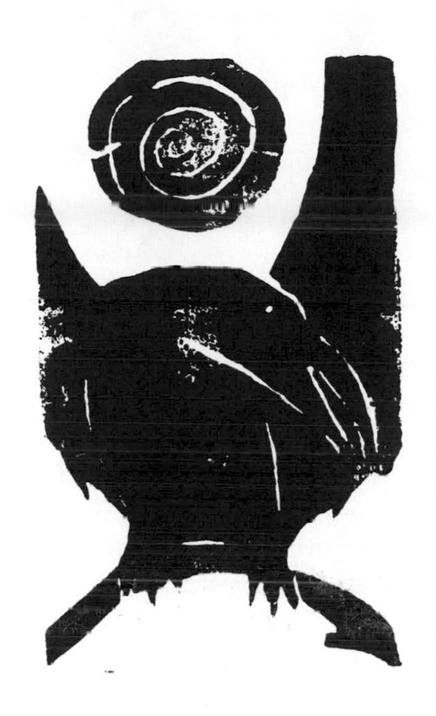

Chapter I

A JUNGIAN THEORETICAL APPROACH TO PSYCHOLOGICAL TRAUMA

"There are moments in human life when a new page is turned."
Jung, "The Psychology of Transference"

C. G. Jung, in his early discussions of the dynamics of the psyche, anticipated much of what we now regard as the symptomatology of posttraumatic stress disorder (PTSD). The more psychological trauma is studied, the more students of behavior come to understand that the problem is universal and pervasive within our culture. We have come to recognize the physiology of the trauma response, and we now realize that much of what we thought was aberrant behavior and mental illness is, in its origin, traumatic (see, for example, recent discussions of physical pain manifesting as PTSD, such as, Cavenar, Nash and Maltbie 1978; Carmen, Rieker and Mills 1984; Benedikt and Kolb, 1986; Rapaport 1987; Walker et al. 1988; and Terr 1990a).

Since I have been interested in psychological trauma for the last ten years, I have come to add questions to my first-interview history survey in order to snare the many sources of today's traumas:

"Was there anything unusual about your birth?"

"Did you have any *unusual* illnesses or injuries in childhood?"

"How were you disciplined?"

"Did you have any life-threatening experiences?"

"Were you ever sexually mistreated?"

"What is the worst thing that ever happened to you?"

I have found that these questions pick up experiences of psychological trauma that would otherwise not be reported because they fall into classes of trauma that are (more or less) natural or at least common and considered unremarkable. The importance of these traumas which are couched in development tends to be downplayed by everyone concerned. The symptoms of such traumata can be ambiguous and given to misattribution by parents and clinicians. This is particularly true for neonatal and early childhood traumas.

The signs and symptoms that lead to a diagnosis of post-traumatic stress disorder, according to the diagnostic manual of the American Psychiatric Association, DSM-IIIR, are useful, certainly, but limited. PTSD as a diagnostic category gives practitioners a chance to agree on what we mean by psychological trauma and its sequelae; but it is a mistake to pretend that where the categorical minimums are not met, psychological trauma disorder does not exist. For instance, when psychological trauma occurs very early in life, symptoms occur out of context, having no ideatic or cognitive frame of reference (van der Kolk and van der Hart 1989).

> Thus, in the first few years of life only the quality of events, but not their context, is remembered. Even after that, the hippocampal localization system remains vulnerable to disruption: severe or prolonged stress can suppress hippocampal functioning . . . creating context free fearful associations that are hard to locate in space and time. This results in amnesia for specifics of traumatic experiences but not the feelings associated with them. (Ibid., p. 1535)

Neonatal surgery and birth crisis (perhaps even trauma to the mother transmitted to the fetus in the late stages of pregnancy) create psychological trauma sequelae that have to do with physiological reexperiencing, particularly the hyperarousal of the emergency responses.

Hypervigilance in the child, running away from home or school, distracting behaviors, and emotional numbing are, together with substance abuse, the avoidance symptoms that we now connect with the nosology of PTSD. One could also argue that adolescent religiosity and obsessive-compulsive schoolwork are manifestations of trauma coping: one occasionally reads of the "A" student who commits a bizarre act that is "out of context" with his or her life-style. Terr (1990a) makes a substantial case for trauma-surviving children as diligent students.

Because of the rapid development of the child, the symptoms of psychological trauma are joined by association almost immediately to a wide variety of stimuli, not the least of which are parental and sibling responses to the hyperaroused child, who we see is a trauma survivor whose concentration is erratic and behavior is restless. Very quickly, then, the child's trauma disorder is paired by association with anger, familial disharmony, and the reactions of authority and is met by attempts to quiet the child's responses with potions, dictums, and disciplines that may or may not ameliorate the symptoms. Learning disabilities, the societal labeling of "incorrigible," and other stigmas that are secondary behaviors have become paired to the hyperarousal state of trauma repetition. These, along with the PTSD symptom of futurelessness, all lead to the misdiagnoses we have come to expect from reviewing the records of child-abuse survivors.

The Trauma Complex

A good theoretical approach that is broad enough to incorporate a full understanding of the developing symptoms of psychological trauma is provided by C. G. Jung. Influenced by Janet, Charcot, Freud, and other nineteenth-century psychodynamic theorists, Jung formulated a concept termed "the feeling-toned complex," which has proved to be robust and helpful in understanding the dynamics of psychological trauma (see Jung 1907, 1928, 1948a, b, and c). Jung's theory is helpful because it predicts behavior from psychological traumata as well as accounting for accidental associations and secondary symptoms that become associated with the trauma response.

Jung took the term *complex* from the Latin verb *complector,* meaning "to encircle, envelope, embrace, take possession of," and the Latin noun *complexus,* which means "mutual entwinement" (Meier 1984, p. 172). Jung theorized that the complex "consists of a nuclear element [the response to the traumatic event] and a large number of secondarily constellated assocations" (1948a, par. 18). Complexes would not originate only from psychological trauma. Other complexes could originate from highly emotional experiences, especially those often repeated. Complex theory might well be termed The Psychology of Big Experiences. Thus parents and other family members and intimate friends, as well as habits and repeated experiences salient enough to form neuronal networks, form prominent complexes in a child's psychological development. Jung thought of the ego identity itself as a complex which forms through associations to body sensations and self-perceptions (1948c, par. 582).

To illustrate Jung's theory, imagine a case of a botched forceps delivery in which the shoulder muscle of the male infant is damaged. The child's arm never gains full strength or growth, and as a boy, he is forced to forego certain activities. Competitive games become painful and demeaning trials to be avoided. The child develops a particularly sharp anger reaction that reaches its peak in high school, where he is finally disciplined and part of his identity is suppressed. The anger is gradually replaced in adulthood by an anxiety (which is usually nocturnal) that he experiences as overwhelming. It is purely physical and has no ideational or imaginal content, except that it seems that he is threatened with total annihilation or madness, although he knows logically that he is not. He notes that the anxiety response is often elicited when he is given challenging creative tasks that require him to leap, as it were, into the unknown. In this fashion, his trauma complex absorbs associations as the individual develops.

An important ingredient in Jung's theory is the concept of the trauma complex as a living, dynamic entity that grows through associations, causing reactions that go far beyond and often obscure the original psychological trauma. Understanding the trauma complex of someone with multiple childhood traumas then becomes a case of carefully mapping the cues and associations in feelings and images, including tangential thoughts and emotions, that arise when the trauma complex is elicited. This is no simple task. For example, for someone who grew up with many traumas that occurred in the home, the cues eliciting the trauma complex are in every room in the house, causing emotional tension, overreaction and dissociation. Thus, one can have the parent who is a survivor of domestic traumas, who is a mean, erratic person at home, where the trauma cues are, and a good person in public, where they aren't.

To further complicate matters, Jung conceived of the complex as resting quietly, as if nonexistent, when not elicited (1948b, par. 201). This can create an enigma in the doctor's office when the patient displays none of the trauma-linked behaviors that are observed by others, much like the malfunctioning automobile that runs well in the repair shop. Many persons with wartime traumas live their lives carefully avoiding matters having to do with warfare. However, loss and death are usually associated with their traumas and these emotional associations are likely to elicit the trauma complex even if it has been quiet for years. Thus, someone who has appeared well adjusted can, at the loss of job, health, or family member, rapidly deteriorate emotionally. Jung writes: "An active complex puts us momentarily under a state of duress of compulsive thinking and acting . . ." (1948b, par. 200). Elsewhere he states (with obvious allusion to wartime trauma) that the trauma complex's

> autonomy consists in its power to manifest itself independently of the will and even in direct opposition to conscious tendencies: it forces itself tyrannically upon the conscious mind. The explosion of affect is a complete invasion of the individual, it pounces upon him like an enemy or wild animal. (1928, par. 267)

It is important to realize that the trauma response is both a conditioned response (Pitman (1989) refers to it as "super conditioning") and an endogenous psychophysiological reaction originating in midbrain (what Edelman (1992) refers to as "primary consciousness"). The trauma response is capable of being elicited by REM sleep state (Ross et al. 1989) and by outside events. It can thus occur and be associated with thoughts and emotions that are internal and value-laden. A survivor of violent trauma can experience a repetition of the hyperarousal state, associate it with anger, and lash out at the nearest person, yet be in total confusion as to why the anger is occurring. For example, it is not uncommon for someone driving on an expressway to have an experience which makes him or her aware that someone could have been killed. This life-threatening emotion cues the trauma complex which results in a rage reaction that is released because it is contained within the "second skin" of the automobile.

When we think of the human brain as a one-kilogram organ so densely packed that it contains 100 billion neurons, more or less, each with up to 15,000 connections (Kolb 1989), we begin to appreciate how one cue, internal or external, can elicit a dynamic pattern of associations that are multidimensional, like a hologram, and that follow predictable pathways. Edelman's theory of neural group selection (1992, pp. 85–87) presents a picture of primary consciousness interacting with maps of neuronal groups in a complex pattern of "reentry" exchange. As Edelman observes, the human mind is more like a jungle than a computer.

Sno and Linszen (1990) give an illustration of the cuing process of hologram memory: "So, in principle, even the smallest fragment would give the complete picture, although the smaller the fragment the less sharp the picture would be" (p. 1593). Thus, to cue a hologram memory the fragment does not have to be precise. Rosenzweig (1988) presents an example of seasonal weather cuing trauma memory that was dissociated and recalled during Mortin Prince's treatment of a patient. In a similiar vein, a signal from one sense could activate several neuronal maps creating the psychic event that Jung referred to as the complex.

Dissociation, itself, as a response to trauma is a natural adaptation that has proven useful in the evolution of the species. Cazzaniga (1989) describes the modular functioning of the brain that has led both to specialization of brain function and to sophisticated overlapping of functions. Dissociation is a process of dispersing brain function in response to environmental demands. Psychodynamically, dissociation is a way to cope with traumatic events leading to resilience in coping with and even preventing posttraumatic sequelae. One dissociative response is to store experience permanently in a safe and inaccessible location. Moments of psychological trauma may derive their amnesia from actual synaptic breaks caused by shock. Dissociation may be a defense against that shock. Then, as Cazzaniga illustrates, "the (ego's) left brain 'interpreter' constructs theories about these dissociated actions and feelings as it tries to bring order and unity to our conscious lives" (p. 951).

Dissociation and the formation of complexes are probably a direct result of evolutionarily desirable brain specialization. Complexes form special groups of cell maps (neuronal matrices) to deal with complicated characters and interactions, e.g., father, mother, religion, school, etc., and traumatic events, particularly repeating traumas that demand survival strategies.

Mammals are trail-makers and tend to repeat behaviors very likely because of the chemical nature of the brain's neuronal pathways. Synaptic gaps between neurons are bridged by transmitters that (within limits) work more easily the more often they are used. Matrices may connect cells over relatively large distances within the brain, connecting a variety of functional areas. Thus, the emotion of grief to a combat veteran, or the experience of sexual intimidation to a rape survivor, or the threat of being restricted to a survivor of a neonatal incubator would follow a complex of neuronal pathways that will predictably elicit a trauma response. (I will discuss further, in chapters 3, 5, and 8, the habit patterns of the trauma complex.) The hyperarousal state would awaken associations unique to that individual's trauma memories. What Jung referred to as personal unconscious is, in part at least, the unconscious content of dormant complexes composed of these neuronal maps, which are quiet because they are not being constellated. One is, of course, capable of remembering complexes when they are not active, but there is a tendency to repress or minimize the effects of painful or morally unacceptable complexes. Blackouts, alcohol-related or not, can occur when a complex is elicited; behavior that is often regarded as bizarre or compulsive follows, and the action is then repressed and forgotten. Where the traumata are redundant, endogenous opioids are released, and psychological numbing ensues, becoming a prominent aspect of the survivor's repetition cycle. "It ain't nothin' but a feelin', Doc" is a phrase from the Vietnam War that expresses this numbing.

Classes of Trauma

Because a trauma complex can be identified by the associations it comprises, it follows that an individual psychological trauma can be classified according to associations to collective trauma experiences of a similar kind. Psychological traumas can indeed be classified in the most general way by the similar associations that they have, given the levels of intensity at which they occur.

Class A: Neonatal Trauma

This class of trauma may proceed from heroic surgical procedures, birth crises, accidents in infancy, abandonment, or other traumatic mistreatment during the first year of life. This is a distinct category due to the formative nature and lack of ideatic imagery or cognitive response. Potential for traumas in neonatal intensive care include high levels of constant fluorescent light, noise, punctures, burns, rough handling, sleep disturbed up to 132 times per day (much of the disturbance for painful procedures), electrical shocks, radiation from 30 to 50 x-rays, long periods in physical restraints for catheterization, and excessive drug administration (Peabody and Lewis 1985). As mentioned earlier, traumatic recall at this age tends to be without context, i.e., hyperarousal only. Only recently has evidence been produced to discount the long-held belief that infants could not be given deep anesthesia during surgery (Anand and Hickey 1992; Rogers 1992).

Class B: Loss Trauma

Abandonment by parents or care-givers, traumatic parental death, and unprepared loss of other significant attachments that radically alters identity are included in this class. (The example of Snow White as mother-abandoned will be discussed in chapter 6.) Testing the limits of tolerance in others in authority or potential intimacy is the remarkable symptom of this class. I have encountered men from the Vietnam War who were abandoned by their units in the bush. For them, loss trauma interacts with other combat traumas. Because treatment does not begin until trust is established, when death interacts with the question of trust, testing takes on a seriousness and intensity that becomes dangerous. The therapist is well-advised to exercise caution when abandonment is a treatment issue.

Class C: Accident Trauma

Where psychological trauma results from vehicular, industrial, or domestic accidents, the symptoms are affected by the survivor's perception of several factors: the role played by others, whether the accident was the result of carelessness or neglect, and the role played by the survivor's own unconscious actions, given the meaningfulness of the accident. Where deaths of others or damages are involved, the survivor's guilt becomes a factor in the symptoms. (Terr 1989b gives excellent examples of the symptoms arising from accident trauma.)

Class D: Sexual Trauma

Incest, rape, and general traumatic sexual mistreatment form a distinct category because of the involvement of sexual associations with autonomic hyperarousal, and the consequent gender-specific development of PTSD symptoms. Guilt and somatic symptoms (body memory), particularly for traumas of early onset, are common. The betrayal of trust is often involved and produces significant issues in psychotherapy (see chapter 7, and also Damlouji and Ferguson (1985), Beck and van der Kolk (1987), and Terr (1990b) for examples of childhood sexual trauma symptoms in adulthood).

Class E: Interpersonal Violence

Child abuse, traumatic application of discipline, spousal battering, life-threatening assaults, and torture are included in this class. The witnessing of interpersonal violence is also included. Anger is the outstanding symptom of this class. Guilt, identification with the perpetrator, and initiating self-harm are symptoms for the survivor and the witness alike (see chapter 8 in this book, and also van der Kolk (1989) and Terr's section on "close encounters" (1990a)).

Class F: Natural Trauma

So-called acts of God, earthquakes, floods, other collective and personal disasters involving loss of community, multiple deaths and impairments, epidemics, overwhelming individual illnesses and medical interventions, including emergency rescue procedures, are all included in this class. "Surgical awareness trauma," in which the patient becomes conscious during surgery but is unable to signal the doctor, would apply here (Owens et al. 1989). Surgical procedures performed on children can be traumatic; Levy (1945) was ahead of his time reporting on the psychological trauma of certain medical procedures. Natural traumas lead to symptomatic association to natural events, e.g., sleepless nights during rainstorms. Robert Louis Stevenson is an excellent example of lifelong illness producing trauma symptoms (see chapter 5). Terr (1987) presents Edith Wharton as an example of this class of trauma. Jung's theory of complexes would make a distinction between the anger associated with a disastrous accident like the slag dam flood at Buffalo Creek, West Virginia (Stern 1976), and a natural disaster like a tornado.

Class G: Combat Trauma

This includes ongoing collective violence and civil unrest where traumatic events are usually multiple and where fatigue and collective emotional contagion prevail and traumatic events take on historic meaning. This class also includes imprisonment during wartime. Anniversary dates of traumas and subtle cues tend to be obscured by the multiplicity of traumas in this class and psychological numbing is a remarkable symptom. Furthermore, some survivors have such a long history of birth trauma, childhood violent and sexual traumata, together with various adult-onset traumas, that they appear for all clinical purposes like combat survivors.

Levels of Psychological Trauma

A somewhat overlapping nosology of trauma refers to levels of traumatic intensity. Psychological trauma is described as causing autonomic hyperarousal (excitement) from a life-threatening or identity-destroying stimulus that exceeds the brain's ability to cope. It is assumed that the brain copes by means of defenses that become more sophisticated with maturity. It is generally believed that the less consciousness or strength of identity the individual has, the less intense the trauma stimulus needs to be to overwhelm the individual. That is, the less mature the individual, the less the magnitude of threatening stimulus required for psychological trauma to occur. Thus, although levels are described, one must not think so much of a linear arrangement, but rather of circuitous levels within levels within levels, much like Dante's description of hell. A low-intensity trauma can, at the right time, or in a sequence that follows previous traumas, create a trauma response that is beyond the level expected by an objective observer. Thus, in the first four levels listed below, the potential for trauma is high because of crucial developmental transitions in the survivor; in the last four levels, the potential for trauma increases with the intensity of the trauma stimulus. Lenore Terr (1990a, 1991) presents a bi-level trauma breakdown: Type I, single trauma, and Type II, multiple or ongoing traumas. Her system is simpler and more practical than the multilevel system presented here, but for the purposes of exposition, the more complex system is desirable.

Level 1

Essentially a defenseless state, such as that found in the neonate, in which the person is entirely vulnerable and is in need of protection. Consciousness, such as it is, is on the level of body presence, and trauma would result from any insult or invasive procedures that cause persistent pain or the withdrawal of care, which would be perceived at this low level of understanding as threatening to existence. An example would be premature birth requiring prolonged incubator care and invasive procedures that result in "assaults on the person and the dignity of the infant" (Peabody and Lewis 1985, p. 262).

Level 2

An infantile-toddler state in which a person is totally dependent on others for nurturance and protection. Consciousness and identity are beginning. The individual is highly vulnerable to accidental threats of abandonment and invasiveness because of the preverbal condition of this state, which prevents clear articulation or understanding. An example of trauma at this level is the toddler who is accidentally left alone by caregivers at a time when nurturing and comfort are required (Bowlby 1979, p. 142). Another example would be physical punishment that exceeds the toddler's endurance. This period is referred to by some as the first stage of individuation (infant to child) and thus a critical period for trauma (Oldham 1989).

Level 3

Trauma in early childhood, or similarly naive state of consciousness, where trust is high and time perception is distorted. Threats to person are perceived as endless. Fatigue comes quickly and the onset of exhaustion is sudden. The newly conscious identity is vulnerable to being overwhelmed by overstimulation. Primitive identity defenses are denial, dissociation, and repression. Examples of trauma at this level are amply described in Terr's description of the Chowchilla school bus kidnapping (1979, 1990a) and in her study of the trauma memories of children (1988).

Level 4

Psychological trauma at crucial developmental periods of transition and growth, such as adolescence. Traumas occurring during periods of identity change or following periods of loss take on additional meaning, such as trauma from a trusted care-giver. Examples are found in Bowlby's (1988) description of mother loss in adolescent girls. Traumas during times of significant transition tend to take on added salience and can alter the course of the survivor's development, while the same trauma during a time of stability would have a lesser effect.

Level 5

Psychological trauma that is a single event, relatively brief, but life-threatening in nature, and unaccompanied by complications of insult upon injury when the survivor is mistreated. Examples are being momentarily trapped in a house fire or being mugged in the street by an overpowering assailant. Examples are abundant in Terr (1990a) and described as "Type 1 trauma" in Terr (1991).

Level 6

Traumas involved in treatment and care-giving that follow a psychological trauma or severe injury which is otherwise discrete. These tend to be added on to or associated with the original trauma. Examples are having major surgery performed without adequate anesthetic (Anand and Hickey 1992) or having major injury or trauma misdiagnosed or misinterpreted by emergency workers. Examples are found in Symonds (1980) and Titchener's observation that the quality of the first hospital experience after a psychological trauma was "crucial to forstall chronicity" (1970, p. 979). The case of Mary Shelley is an example of this level: she experienced a double loss when her mother died shortly after she was born, then her surrogate mother left her father's employ and abandoned her when she was three years of age (Mellor 1988).

Level 7

Repeating inescapable threats to identity and well-being, psychological traumas following one another in a reasonably contiguous fashion, and recurring threats following psychological traumas, such as harassment threatening repetition of the trauma. Numbing gradually sets in and each successive trauma seems less dramatic, although symptoms tend to accumulate. Examples of this level are found in cases of spousal battering and in societies where racial or ethnic violence is common.

Level 8

Crisis and destruction that continues for months and years, including wartime combat and imprisonment where brutality and cruelty reign and where carnage and suffering are repeatedly witnessed by persons with reduced energy and ability to cope. The Holocaust of the Nazi era is an example. The cultural annihilation of the Native Americans is an ongoing example. A historic example in the Middle Ages was the repeating scourge of the Black Death (Gies and Gies 1987).

Level 9

That state of cataclysm which would overcome everyone, wherein landscape and community are destroyed and humanity is reduced to helplessness. Examples are the Nagasaki and Hiroshima A-bomb explosions.

Treatment Implications of Jungian Theory

The concept of psychological trauma forming a psychic complex that is descrete from the identity of the survivor directs the course of treatment. Jung wrote: "A traumatic complex brings about dissociation of the psyche. The complex is not under the control of the will and for this reason it possesses the quality of psychic autonomy" (1928, par. 266). Abreaction, or the recollection of the trauma event in psychotherapy, then "is an attempt to reintegrate the autonomous complex, to incorporate it *gradually* into the conscious mind as an accepted content by living the traumatic situation over again, once or repeatedly" (ibid., par. 268, my emphasis).

The repression of the psychological trauma decreases available conscious energy. More than just the trauma event is lost; as described earlier, many accidental and secondary associations to the trauma are repressed or avoided as well. When traumas are many or significantly momentous, what remains of the survivor's identity becomes brittle and defensive. For adults, reintegration of the trauma and its associations results in the increase of consciousness and, predictably, self-esteem. In some respects, psychotherapy can help achieve a consciousness that is greater than existed prior to the trauma in question. For children, the treatment issue is less one of acceptance than of interpretation of the trauma complex's influence on the child's behavior.

The Soul Guide

The psychotherapist is, in many respects, like the soul guide found in many hero myths, who takes the protagonist into the underworld, where dead souls reside, to get advice about how to proceed on the quest (e.g., the *Aeneid*, the *Odyssey, The Divine Comedy*). These guides are helpful characters who have knowledge of the underworld but do not themselves discover the useful information. Likewise, the therapist of PTSD does not know the client's trauma-laden material *a priori* but can only stay close to the signposts and take the client as far as he or she wants to go. Once there, the soul guide can help the client only by predictably providing a safe place to explore the material.

When approaching psychological trauma, the therapist should be as cautious as an animal around a strange object. What traumatized one person can contribute to the trauma of another. There are a number of therapies that advocate the rending of the trauma to consciousness through implosion, marathon treatment sessions, videotaped hypnosis, or chemical trance induction and risk a revictimization of the survivor. Similar victimization occurs when the client is forced into an unsuitable treatment regimen because fiscal or administrative institutional policy dictates it. One assumes that the trauma was repressed for good reason and that defenses are protective of the survivor's identity. One therefore approaches the issue at the client's pace, learning as much as one can of the trauma through the client's conscious recall, using nightmares, dreams, intrusive thoughts, and fantasies as signs, attempting to see the trauma as it is revealed through the client's eyes. The therapist regards with respect every occasion of overreaction from the client, either in session or by report, and follows each one back by association to its most significant source.

For instance, a client who was raped on different occasions in her history reports a repeating nightmare of being imprisoned in a dungeon with corpses and body parts. She also has a repeating intrusive fantasy of a beautiful woman in a gown lying dead by suicide, her wrists slashed. She is living in a group home and has an angry confrontation with a male resident when he refuses to assist her with chores. The confrontation raises the memory of earlier domestic fights with her problematic parents. Each of these events is worth amplification in psychotherapy and, if not immediately explored, should at least be stored in the therapist's notes for later referral. Dreams and fantasies, where the imagery permits, can be illustrated with various representational media, resulting in a multilevel dialogue between therapist and client with the purpose of making the autonomous complex more familiar, i.e., rejoining the ego identity. Terr gives an excellent example from her own training of the significance of the repeating dream in trauma therapy (1990a, p. 209). The therapist weaves this material like a coat and returns it to the client, embroidered with the collective heritage of myth, legend, and current scientific literature. In the above example, for instance, the fairy tales "Bluebeard" and "Snow White" might be worth exploring (see chapters 6 and 8).

Some classes of trauma can be treated collectively in a mixture of group and individual psychotherapy, supplemented with case management and chemotherapy. Group therapy works especially well in PTSD treatment when the traumas in question are collective historical events. Even with collective trauma, however, the client should be approached initially on an individual basis and screened for additional treatment issues before placement in a treatment group. It is always important that the therapist understand each client's personal symbols, including the trauma imagery, and develop a sense of how the trauma(s) affects consciousness.

Some group theorists believe the homogeneous group (a therapy group composed of only one kind of trauma survivor) is self-limiting in the treatment of psychological trauma. Such criticism suggests some groups do not succeed, especially if time is limited. But groups of Vietnam veterans or incest survivors are more heterogeneous than they are homogeneous, and if the therapists keep their diversity before them, they will be less likely to stall in their progress.

The therapy group functions as a collective consciousness that contains the members and is stronger than any one of them. It allows the Aesculapian healer (see next chapter) to arise in the group, drawing members outside of themselves and into caring for others, which helps them heal.

The Helpful Animal

Seemingly insignificant details in the report of a psychological trauma in therapy can lead the therapist to a grasp of the trauma's impact on the survivor. Another common motif in fairy tales is the hero or heroine who sets off on an adventure and is met by a relatively insignificant creature—a dwarf, crone, or helpful animal—and, being respectful of the creature's needs, is in return assisted or provided with advice or a talisman. Sometimes the creature becomes a soul guide and leads or helps the protagonist to achieve the desired end. The important message here for the therapist is the concept of respectfully approaching even seemingly insignificant information that is received from the client. The little fish lying on the river bank and gasping for air, if returned to its proper place, may later bring up from the deep the key that unlocks the treasure.

Sometimes a client reports having no significant dreams, only some fleeting images upon waking. Talkative clients may then proceed to obscure these images, which may be far more significant than the wordy recap of the week's interpersonal struggles. One of the symptoms of PTSD is avoidance of trauma recollection, and clients avoid more cleverly and unconsciously than therapists often appreciate. Respecting the humble little character by the roadside can uncover more trauma than comfortable therapeutic patter.

Contamination

Eventually the therapist becomes contaminated by association with the emotions of the psychological trauma. Ambivalence in the client becomes extreme as the client wishes to be healed and also wishes to avoid the therapist associated with the trauma. Transference is problematic for treatment when the traumas involve violence and betrayal of authority or trusted others. Almost all traumas, by definition, involve ignominious, shameful, or guilty associations. Jung's difficult and wonderful essay on transference refers to the Latin *in stercore invenitur*, "it is found in filth" (Jung 1946, par. 384). He refers to the therapeutic liaison as "an unreal intimacy" (ibid., par. 368), eliciting in the client, who is a survivor of psychological trauma, a feeling of vulnerability that can become unbearable. Every problem that exists in the repetition of trauma can possibly be manifested in the therapeutic hour, if only in the emotional process of the client.

Jung likens the struggle of achieving wholeness by making conscious previously unconscious material to the problem of incest. "Incest symbolizes union with one's own being, it means individuation or becoming a self, and, because this is so vitally important, it exerts unholy fascination" (ibid., par. 419). The additional problem faced by the trauma survivor and therapist is the association of painful trauma emotions with the already difficult problems set forth in the individuation process during psychotherapy. This problem becomes immensely complex when the trauma in question is literally one of incest.

In principle, what is in consciousness is differentiated in terms of value. What is unconscious is perforce undifferentiated. The bad contaminates the good in the unconscious, where nature is raw and brutal and collective value has no place. Once trauma material is repressed, the trauma complex operates as a traveler who passes between conscious and unconscious territories. The trauma complex becomes associated with other unconscious contents. Achieving psychological wholeness then becomes a moral dilemma. "Wholeness," writes Jung, "is not so much perfection as completeness" (1946, par. 452). Psychotherapy becomes a process of separating the best from the worst in oneself, and contamination results from contact with that which is taboo.

> It [incest] is the hiding place for all the most secret, painful, intense, delicate, shamefaced, timorous, grotesque, unmoral, and at the same time the most sacred feelings which go to make up the indescribable and inexplicable wealth of human relationships and give them their compelling power. (Ibid., par. 371)

What we often fail to appreciate about psychological trauma is that, to survive such life-threatening events, one is required to do whatever is necessary. From the primitive midbrain come signals of primary consciousness that alarm human passions to assist in the struggle to survive. This is true for the neonate undergoing corrective surgery and the infant who senses abandonment. And while endogenous opioids are blunting the pain, perceptual senses are operating with increased clarity. Although the specific trauma event may be irretrievably forgotten because convulsive shock causes amnesia, the hyperarousal state repeats at a frequency that remains unpredictable. Being in the therapist's office, repeatedly making associations to the trauma events, elicits that state again and again, while the therapist contributes observations that lead to understanding. The client learns how and when the hyperarousal is likely to occur by making conscious its associations. He or she can then learn to dissociate voluntarily from the traumatically reexperienced hyperarousal. By thus dissociating, the client can then decide whether or not to act on the arousal impulse.

Trauma in the Family

If one member of a family is traumatized, chances are the entire family will experience some aspect of the resulting PTSD. While the trauma-stimulated hyperarousal state may repeat for the rest of the survivor's life, understanding how it operates, knowing this process as one knows a trail through the forest, one can separate the traumatogenic aspects from the current context. This is important in preventing psychological trauma from contaminating family members and from being passed through successive generations. Jung observed:

> Anything that falls into the unconscious takes on a more or less archaic form. If, for example, the mother represses a painful and terrifying complex, she will feel it is an evil spirit pursuing her—a "skeleton in the cupboard". . . . It sits on her like an incubus, she is tormented by nightmares. Whether she tells "nightmare stories" to the child or not, she none the less infects the child and awakens in its mind archetypal terror images from her own psychology. (1931, par. 62)

When storytellers talk of spinning a good yarn, they are referring to the female voice in folklore and fairy-tale tradition (Rowe 1986). Mothers or Nannies were the conveyers of trauma tales in the generations before electronic communications, insofar as the tales they selected to pass on were influenced by their own trauma histories.

When I was a child, adventure radio excited images that largely substituted for mother's "nightmare stories," stimulating my imagination. As I will show later in chapter 3, these were collective fantasies from modern culture. In the days of my childhood, they were dramas drawn from the Old West, when the survivors of the U.S. Civil War engaged in skirmishes with Indians and each other. Today, of course, television plays this role, presenting mutants and robots of an urban civilization ruined by technology and at war with itself. Even if children are barred from mass media, they are continuously exposed to the unconscious complexes of their parents, siblings, and friends. As Terr so boldly states: "Psychic trauma is one of the most contagious mental conditions known to psychiatry at this time" (1989a, p. 16).

Psychological trauma can be transmitted from the survivor to other family members either symptomatically, by suggestion, trauma "play" or modeling, or by directly traumatizing the family member.

Symptomatic transmission occurs through specific trauma anxiety, anger, paranoia, or phobia regarding potential trauma sources; avoidance of trauma symptoms or difficult emotions; and drug and alcohol use with all the secondary problems substance abuse creates. Glassman, Magulac and Darko (1987) present a case example of trauma-magnified paranoia infecting the family.

Specific symptoms related to PTSD that affect the family are: overreactive affect, reduced tolerance for stress, emotional isolation, inadequate bonding to children, symbolic repetition of trauma, trauma play, identification with the aggressor, distrust, and testing the limits of tolerance, particularly for those abandoned or abused in early childhood. Obviously trauma can be passed from child to parent, parent to child, spouse to spouse, child to child, etc. (This issue is further discussed in chapters 8 and 9. Terr (1990a) gives extensive examples of trauma play transmission through generations.)

Direct traumatization of family members may occur through violence, excessive discipline, sexual mistreatment, and abandonment. Research by Oliver (1988) shows violence passed through successive generations.

Trauma play and fantasy, more difficult concepts to grasp, involve the unconscious transmission of trauma imagery between spouses or between survivor and child. One spouse may develop an incest fantasy after living with a mate who was traumatized as a child through incest. In the worst cases, the contaminated spouse does not end the process with fantasy images but directly acts out the incest within the family. Terr (1979) describes a younger sibling of a traumatized girl dreaming her sister's trauma dream and illustrates how children unconsciously share trauma experiences through games that continue for generations (1981). She notes that "Ring around the Rosy" still survives as a game passed down from the plagues of medieval Europe. "Hide and Seek" can have an air of traumatic thrill in being lost and found, as noticed by parents whose children hide from them in department stores.

The symptoms of psychological trauma may be transmitted directly by the communication of fear through the overprotection of children, guilt through the traumatized parent's need for revenge or the reestablishment of honor, or by repeated expressions of hatred for the race, ethnicity, gender, or class of the original trauma perpetrator (see deWind 1968; Terr 1989a; Danieli 1985; and Epstein 1981, for a journalist's account).

Coping defenses, originally used to survive trauma, may contribute to the unconscious transmission of psychological trauma. Defenses such as denial and repression lose their original value when played out in family life. For instance, the emotional compartmentalization of trauma memories, when they produce lapses or blocks in consciousness and moral character, lead to behavior that is unrecognized or unappreciated for its meaning and implication.

Three general examples illustrate the interfamilial transmission of psychological trauma.

Example A

The combat veteran father who refuses to discuss his war experiences, leading his son to develop a fascination for war and a need to prove himself to his withdrawn and unexpressive father (see Rosenheck 1986, for a case example). This process conveys the message that the child cannot handle the trauma material and is thus inadequate, leading to a veritable grail quest to seek the forbidden. A variation of this theme is seen in the sexually traumatized parent who bans discussion of sex, leading to a mystery that enlarges the importance of the subject and increases the potential for naive exploration on the part of the children.

Example B

The parent who displays hysterical tantrums of anger or sexual misbehavior while intoxicated or fatigued, tantrums that are subsequently not remembered (the original trauma having been dissociated) and which thus remain unintegrated for both trauma survivor and family, and serve as a model for the future behavior of children. Any attempts by the other family members to discuss or confront the survivor result in fits of overreactive affect, rage, tearful denunciation, helplessness, depression, or suicidal behavior that is usually symbolic of the original trauma events. (See the film *Desert Bloom*, directed by Eugene Corr, for an excellent dramatization of this example; Spiegel (1988) for a discussion of dissociation in trauma; and Krystal (1978) for examples of overreactive affect in the family.)

Example C

Identification with the aggressor by which the survivor becomes better at domination, or better at business, or more aggressive, or otherwise overcompensates for the trauma perpetrator's power. Engaging in overwork, never being weak, becoming emotionally insulated and brittle, or otherwise emotionally neglecting, dominating, or impoverishing one's family as a result of a trauma symptom. (See Soloman, Kotler and Mikulincer (1988) for an example of guilt affecting Israeli soldiers whose parents survived the Holocaust.)

Summary

Fairy tales and myths do not necessarily deal directly with recovery from psychological trauma, but they often deal with the problem of achieving psychological wholeness, which is the ultimate problem for trauma recovery. The survivor who has successfully integrated the trauma complex is conscious of its manifestations and is therefore able to exercise an additional amount of conscious control. If the trauma itself is sufficiently strong, the trauma complex continues to exert its influence for the rest of the survivor's life. It is apparent, however, that after midlife the locus ceruleus (the habitat of Pan) declines in potency (Roose and Pardes 1989). With the decline of the locus ceruleus, the trauma complex may become less influential as far as disturbing concentration and influencing behavior. However, with traumas of high levels of intensity, the influence of the trauma complex sets one back in one's development, sometimes delaying physical and emotional growth for years, and continues to death and beyond via the influence passed on in the family and culture.

The therapist's goal is to teach the survivor to recognize the trauma complex, predict its manifestations, and mitigate and redirect its influence. One of the reasons fairy tales like "Cinderella," "Snow White," "Bluebeard," "Hansel and Gretel," "Little Red Riding Hood," "Bearskin," and "Donkey Skin" are so popular across cultures and through generations is that they express fundamental human problems created by psychological traumas: deaths of parents, abandonment, spousal abuse, war, incest, rape . . . the confrontation of the worst that is in oneself and in the world. By using the relevant products of the culture together with the material provided by the survivor, the therapist can conceptualize the problems presented by the trauma complex in a manner that is both unique to the individual and general to the problems of humanity. It is a very lucky person who survives a lifetime without psychological trauma, but it is quite possible to survive the worst of psychological trauma with good and persistent psychotherapy.

The chief ingredient of psychotherapy with a trauma survivor is the understanding and use of countertransference. The next chapter will illustrate the dimensions of countertransference images of a therapist working with trauma disorder.

Chapter

2

UNWANTED CONSCIOUSNESS
Countertransference and Culture

The use of psychotherapy in the treatment of PTSD is appropriate across all classes of psychological trauma and requires, among other things, the development of a trusting relationship between the therapist and the trauma survivor. Such a relationship is usually emotionally intense, activating fantasies in both client and therapist. As a psychologist, I have learned to pay attention to my fantasies and learn what I can from them. I wish to describe here the images that were stimulated in my fantasy as a psychotherapist working with trauma survivors, and the understanding the fantasies have given to me of the nature of trauma disorder and its treatment.

Psychological trauma is that moment in life when, as Jung wrote, "a new page is turned" (1946, par. 373). In 1979, when I began doing psychotherapy with war veterans, I experienced an explosion of images in my mind. I likened it to tossing an object into a campfire and watching the sparks fly. Although I knew when I started working with Vietnam veterans that I was getting in touch with society's shadow and would be contaminated, I did not appreciate that I was stepping into an archetypal situation which had repeated over centuries. The sparks stimulated in my imagination were the age-old trauma images of my Celtic past and its mythology, Western classical mythology, my own popular-culture myths, and the mythic images of

Native Americans indigenous to the Pacific Northwest. Some of the images I recalled from my own middle American culture: the heroes from the Old West of movies and radio, superheroes from comics and folklore. These were all countertransference images waiting, like wayside gnomes, to offer me meaning when I recognized them. At that time, the most prominent of the images was that of the raven: the Celtic warrior raven, Goethe's raven who was the devil's messenger, and the Northwest native image of "Raven-Who-Makes-Things-Right" (Martin 1951).

Raven Images

In the Northwest Native American myth, Raven, responding to the plight of people living in darkness, steals the light from the giant or spirit people, where it was kept hidden in a box, and brings light to man. He does this in various ways, depending on the source of the story. In some stories, he manages to steal the light by deception, gaining entrance by posing as a slave, by getting swallowed and impregnating the virgin daughter, or by hiding in someone's orifice. Raven, who has been white up to this time, is turned black when he flies up through the smoke hole of the light keeper's hut to escape. Raven is a creation hero, bringing the sun and the stars and the moon, all sources of our light, to man and scattering the lot in the heavens.

Raven as trickster and sun-messenger god comes from several sources (Reid and Bringhurst 1984; de Armond 1975). The images of Raven are common on the Northwest coast of Canada and the United States and are even depicted on the shoulder patch of the Washington National Guard (the 81st Mechanized Infantry Brigade).

The association of the raven with death comes naturally from the efficiency of ravens (*Corvus corax*) as carrion eaters. From the earliest times of human history, ravens have followed warriors into battle for the same reason they followed hunters and wolf packs—to feast on the corpses. Their association with death made them harbingers (Heinrich 1989). My own Celtic version of Raven was as the triune goddess of war:

the Morrigan, Macha, and Badb (Rees and Rees 1961). The Celtic warrior knew "the way of the black ravens" (Markale 1975, p. 58).

I was also familiar with the ravens in Goethe's *Faust* as Mephistopheles' messengers, a reminder of the Western bias of raven as shadow. I knew of Raven as a rank in Mithra, the mystery religion popular among the soldiers of Imperial Rome, and I also knew of Poe's image of raven as "Croak of doom" and symbol for his traumatic loss (Terr 1987, p. 520).

The way in which Raven becomes black in Northwest native myth is given similar treatment in Ovid's *Metamorphoses*, where raven is turned black by Apollo for bringing him unwanted news. Raven tells Apollo that he saw his mortal girlfriend, Coronis, having sex with a man. Apollo kills Coronis with an arrow and snatches his son, Aesculapius, out of her womb and gives him to the centaur, Chiron, to raise. "As for the raven," Ovid writes, "Whose report was right and hopes ran high, he turned him black as night . . ." (*Metamorphoses* 2. 634–635).

Jung (1944) associates Ovid's version with the myth of Diana and Actaeon, in which the hunter Actaeon accidentally witnesses Diana bathing and is turned into a stag to be killed by his own dogs. Dogs are sacred to Diana/Artemis and an important symbol of the goddess's dark side. Ovid recounts a tale which predates patriarchy. In another version of this theme, Tiresias saw Athena bathing and was struck blind, but the goddess gave Tiresias the power of divination by understanding the language of birds. There are many other versions of mortals being devastated by visions of the divine. Semele, daughter of Cadmus and Harmonia and mother of Dionysus, had sexual liaison with Zeus and was deceived by Hera/Juno into demanding to see Zeus's divinity. She was turned into ashes by the sight. Her son, Dionysus, was the only Greek god with a human mother. He was immortalized by being "reborn" by Zeus. Dionysus eventually rescued his mother from Hades. Dionysus is associated with other suffering and wandering gods, such as Osiris before him and Christ, whose religion later subsumed much of his imagery.

Trauma Survivor as Raven

These raven stories of unwanted consciousness are relevant to the trauma survivor, who, as bearer of bad news, becomes the raven, who turns black with trauma consciousness, i.e., opprobrium, isolation, and guilt. The news, of course, is the trauma experience, a unique awareness of nature's brutality in conjunction with extreme physical arousal (panic) and dissociation.

The images of trauma have a physical base, common to both survivor and therapist. Jung's description of the process of trauma disorder as psychic complex fits quite well with what we now think of as cortical maps. Lawrence Kolb recently described the physical reaction to trauma:

> With excessive cortical sensitization and diminished capacity for habituation of the agonistic neuronal system, lower brain stem structures, such as the medial hypothalamic nuclei and the locus ceruleus, activated by the neurotransmitter norepinephrine, escape from inhibitory cortical control. Through their extensive cortical and subcortical connections, they, in turn, repeatedly reactivate the perceptual, cognitive, affective, and somatic clinical expressions related to the original traumata. Thus, in the face of perceived threats there occurs excessive sympathetic arousal—including neuroendocrine disturbances as well as behavioral expressions of rage and irritability and repetitive cortical reactivation of memories related to the traumatic event. The latter are projected in the daytime as intrusive thoughts and at nighttime in the recurrent traumatic nightmares of posttraumatic stress disorder in all forms. (Kolb 1987, p. 989)

Kolb describes a process of trauma that repeats in the survivor: a physical excitation flowing from midbrain to cortex that is experienced as a repetition of images and emotions associated with the trauma, becoming trauma consciousness. Ross and associates (1989) link the repetition of trauma disturbance to REM state. Compare these modern descriptions to Jung's early description of a trauma complex:

> For the trauma is either a single, definite, violent impact, or a complex of ideas and emotions which may be likened to a psy-

> chic wound. Everything that touches this complex, however slightly, excites a vehement reaction, a regular emotional explosion. Hence one could easily represent the trauma as a complex with a highly emotional charge. (Jung 1928, par. 262)

Trauma consciousness consists of the images of the trauma and associated emotions, charged and confused memories, which the survivor is unable to repress completely and struggles to integrate. Each survivor's trauma consciousness is uniquely his or her own and difficult to recall accurately, let alone share with others. What turns the survivor black is his or her own consciousness of what has happened. Trauma consciousness is unique to the individual and is shared by no other, leading to anonymity symbolized by blackness, rather like the black Dionysian mask on the Lone Ranger (the Lone Ranger as Dionysus will be discussed further in chapter 3). The modern cinema "strong men," such as John Wayne and Clint Eastwood and their European and Asian counterparts, are culture heros played to stereotypes of the haunted, emotionally repressed trauma survivor, which probably developed from the sensational journalistic accounts of the wandering Civil War survivor.

Trauma Complex as Healing Resource

What is important about Ovid's version of how the raven becomes black is that, as the result of the deed, Apollo gives the gift of healing to the infant Aesculapius. Apollo wounds the infant by snatching him from Coronis's body; thus, in her death, Coronis gives birth to the wounded healer. Consistent with the myth, I have found in the treatment of trauma survivors that understanding the trauma, "knowing" one's trauma complex the way one knows a familiar trail, can produce empathy by leading one into newfound spirituality. Unwanted consciousness, if not repressed, leads to personality growth and a potentially "higher" consciousness. However, by definition, the pain of a psychic trauma is such that the complex cannot be, at least initially, fully conscious.

One defines the trauma complex phenomenologically by studying the ways it manifests as a conditioned response in overreactive affect, fascination, intrusive imagery, anxiety, nightmares, and shifts in mood. The trauma complex, because it is probably never fully known, then becomes a channel or tunnel to the unconscious, like the Lone Ranger's silver mine, a renewable source of riches. By knowing the action of the trauma complex, the survivor can potentially mine the tunnel, as it were, and know himself or herself more completely than one who was not traumatized.

The figure of Coronis in Ovid's raven story is interesting. The goddesses associated with Coronis are Artemis or Diana. Coronis is the dark aspect of the moon goddess, the Black Virgin or Crow Maiden (Jung 1944). Graves, however, referring to more primitive sources, equates Coronis directly with Athena, to whom the crow was sacred (Graves 1948, p. 51). This confusion becomes resolved only if one thinks of the goddesses as evolving from one moon goddess. As such she is also the Lady of the Beasts (Neumann 1963) and in her dark side represents the bestial side of nature. To view the goddess naked is to view the unconscious and the body's primitive resources unprepared. What turns the raven black or Actaeon into a stag is the knowledge of the bestial and the impact of the potency (divinity) of nature. It is also that consciousness that opens a stream of energy from the unconscious, because one also, by the experience, has a hint of the full potency of oneself. "The holiest shudder comes not from the tremendous and infinitely powerful, but rather from the depths of natural experience," wrote Walter Otto in *The Homeric Gods* (1954, p. 9). Every trauma experience is thus archetypal. Ovid emphasizes the potency of nature by the crow's warning stories, when the crow tries to dissuade raven from carrying the news to Apollo. We are told stories of rape, rage-filled murder, and incest, the point being that the worst of nature begets the worst, i.e., psychic trauma.

The mythological motif described thus far, the mortal who is devastated as a result of viewing the goddess, is presented in a variant form in the Grimms' fairy tale "Goosegirl at the Well." In the Grimms' tale, the divinity of the goddess is implied by the maiden washing herself in the moonlight, viewed by a man hiding in a tree. The man is a nobleman searching for a witch who has been harboring a princess. The princess has been disguised as an ugly goosegirl after being cast out by her father. But when the nobleman finally sees the goosegirl bathing in the moonlight, he sees her in her undisguised beauty.

> But how astonished he was, when she went to the well, took off the [ugly] skin and washed herself, when her golden hair fell down all about her, and she was more beautiful than anyone whom he had ever seen in the whole world. He hardly dared to breathe, but stretched his head as far forward through the leaves as he could, and stared at her. Either he bent over too far, or whatever the cause might be, the bough suddenly cracked and that very moment the maiden slipped into the skin, sprang away like a roe, and as the moon was suddenly covered, disappeared from his sight. (Grimm and Grimm 1972, p. 732)

This theme of the goddess in disguise is further explored in chapter 5. The importance of the theme here is to emphasize the dangerous aspect of psychological trauma, when one is overwhelmed by the experience of the unexpected.

Posttraumatic Recovery

Another representation of the raven's blackness is found in the Grimms' fairy tales describing the discharged war veteran. In two of these stories, "The Devil's Sooty Brother" and "Bearskin," the devil approaches the veteran, who is abject and helpless to save himself upon his discharge from the army. The devil promises material wealth in exchange for seven years of servitude (perhaps implying seven years' growth to consciousness), during which time the war veteran has to refrain from self-care. He must cut neither his fingernails nor his hair, nor shave nor wash. In "Bearskin," he must wear the skin of a bear that he has killed to prove his courage.

The bear is sacred to Diana/Artemis. Zeus, in love with the nymph Callisto, disguised himself as Artemis and by the deception seduced Callisto. Zeus later turned Callisto into a bear to escape the moon goddess's pointed wrath.

The Grimms' tales are European Christianized folk and fairy stories gathered by the brothers in the nineteenth century. The devil has aspects of pagan vegetation deities. The cloven hooves belong to the goat-god of natural instinct, Pan, as well as to Dionysus, Lord of the Underworld, who was once turned into a goat by Zeus and was worshiped in that image. Recall Dionysus's role in saving his mother, Semele, who was also devastated by the sight of a god, even though she "asked for it." She was deceived by Hera, disguised as an old woman, to ask to see Zeus's divinity. Semele, it could be said, like many war veterans, volunteered, but not for trauma disorder. The image of Dionysus connected with the war survivor, or indeed any trauma survivor, is fitting. His cult observance was one of death, dismemberment, and resurrection. As the suffering god with a human mother, he is also associated with Christ. Trauma survivors seem to be drafted into his cult automatically. The war survivor, besides witnessing death, dismemberment, and his own resurrection as a survivor quite literally, also experiences the plight of the trauma survivor in general, which involves the threat of death, the repression of the trauma experience, effectively cutting off part of his or her consciousness, and finally, hopefully, the reintegration of consciousness with healing. Aesculapius then becomes a healing aspect of Dionysus, Lord of the Underworld (Graves 1948, p. 51).

Bearskin's devil in a green coat, also known as Lord of the Underworld, recalls the medieval Celtic legends from the Mabinogion, and later "Sir Gawain and the Green Knight," in which the giant figure of death appears in the form of a green primitive hero (Zimmer 1971). Robin Hood's green apparel is also a mark of a vegetation deity and a kind of male version of Artemis and her nymphs. Maid Marian as sea goddess (Graves 1948, p. 395) associates Robin with Dionysus.

Death as a green vegetation deity gradually evolved into death as Grim Reaper. The Lone Ranger in black mask with silver quickness is also a Dionysian figure, particularly in the Lone Ranger's suffering in isolation in the cave, followed by his resurrection as a wandering hero. The Lone Ranger is, in this sense, the ego's sun hero who descends into the underworld as the result of trauma and comes under the authority of the moon goddess in her dark phase, e.g., the Black Virgin.

In these stories the hero is tested with the threat of death, the trials of poverty, pain, and isolation. Gawain, on his journey to pay his debt to the Green Knight, like the war veterans in Grimms' stories, is challenged to endure the opprobrium of the wandering beast. The Northwest native raven trickster stories incorporate the wandering fool and the hero in one figure, similar to other Native American tricksters (Radin 1972).

It is this period of painful test, signifying the battle for consciousness, that I think represents the worst experiences of post-trauma response. This is the period of acute posttraumatic stress disorder, when the trauma complex is at its most disruptive, imposing isolated alienation, self-inflicted humiliations, paranoia, anhedonia, fear, grief, irrational anger, and painful memories.

There follows potentially then a period of posttraumatic adjustment, a liminal state of trickster behavior in which costume and shape changes describe alterations in the personality dynamically energized by trauma. The trauma complex creates a channel of activating energy from unconscious nature to ego consciousness, perhaps, as Ross and associates (1989) speculate, along a REM pathway. This is a time of brilliance and foolishness, roughly comparable to the adolescent state, when mistakes are made and emotions erupt, a time of uncanny intuition and romantic, sad, haunting moments of déjà vu. The term *liminal* refers to Victor Turner's work, *The Ritual Process,* examining initiation rituals in which "the underling comes uppermost" (1969, p. 102).

The reward of release from the chthonic deity's obligation is won gradually with repeated regression as the contents of the trauma complex are gradually absorbed into consciousness. The reward is a higher consciousness represented as riches, as handsomeness and status, as healing power, and as knightly purity, describing the ego that has contact with expanded consciousness and has begun the process of integrating the trauma-induced, crude elements of nature that are brought to light from the dark unconscious. In "Bearskin" and "Goosegirl at the Well" (and, as we will later see, in "Donkey Skin"), the wholeness is represented by the ritual cleaning of the body, the handsome carriage with four white horses, and the acceptance by the betrothal to the youngest daughter upon combining the ring halves. The introduction of the youngest daughter is the mirror image to the trauma fairy tale from the feminine point of view, such as "Cinderella." In the feminine version, wholeness is represented by the fancy dress, the carriage, and the union with the prince.

For Bearskin to change he must have a relationship with the youngest daughter, who represents creative adaptation, the role played by Aesculapius in Ovid. The trauma survivor must wrest part of his or her trauma from the unconscious to serve the conscious ego. Joseph Henderson, in his essay on the bear, refers to the rite of the Great Mother, in which

> the initiant felt himself transformed into an animal and so underwent a sacrifice, but also a process of regeneration. By submitting to the death-dealing power of the goddess, he experienced rebirth *as an animal*. For he can experience upon an animal level, and the quality which is thus acquired is expressed archetypally as *vis ut sis*. Practically speaking, the bear ritual points to integration of the new personality following such a period of dissociation. (Henderson 1967, pp. 230–231)

Summary

Consciousness, wanted or not, seeks to increase as any animate product of nature seeks to grow. The problems created by dissociation and repression in trauma disorder mimic the normal development of ego in the growth of consciousness. What can be learned from myths, legends, folk tales, and other popular products of our culture is the perspective that gives sense, meaning, and direction in our approach to the trauma recovery process. In chapter 3 we will examine one folk hero, the Lone Ranger, and see how the repetition experience accommodates serial adventure shows.

Anybody can be traumatized, young or old, dull or quick-witted, and the survivor seeking treatment often will be uninterested in academic and mythical references. It is crucial, however, that the therapist be sensitive to his or her own cultural heritage and keep an inner ear to the images activated in treating trauma survivors. Countertransference in the psychotherapy of trauma survivors is a mythical stream. The fact that psychic trauma is always an archetypal experience dramatizes and intensifies the therapist's work. Each trauma survivor witnesses the god or goddess (brutal nature) unprepared, and each therapist, as healer, becomes the stumbling wounded healer assisting the survivor. Especially in the PTSD treatment group, the survivors themselves come to value their own healing capacities and, as wounded healers, heal their own trauma wounds in the process of caring for others.

On a Fiery Horse Chapter 3

The Lone Ranger as Sun Hero and Trauma Survivor

"In the ranger's eyes there was a light that must have burned in the eyes of the knights in armor: a light that through the ages lifted the souls of strong men who fought for justice—for God. 'I'll be the Lone Ranger.'"

The Lone Ranger is one of several popular heroes who change into stronger characters as the result of trauma. Like his predecessors, Zorro and the Scarlet Pimpernel, the Lone Ranger was created for wide public appeal. Although the Lone Ranger was created without the benefit of modern psychology, the imagery depicted aptly describes the trauma experience.

Trauma to the psyche involves being made helpless and overwhelmed, often with the threat of death, and generates the energy of full emergency arousal, grossly overstimulating the brain. Like Huck Finn setting off on the Mississippi raft with Jim, the trauma survivor is launched into an archetypal river without control. Described by Jung (1956) as the experience of the sun hero in the underworld, the quest to restore the psyche's wholeness depicts the ego's Promethean experience as it fights to wrest light from chaotic darkness. Every age in our culture seems to create a sun hero legend with its own cultural trappings. In the mythology of contemporary North America, the popular radio and television legend of the Lone Ranger describes the sun hero in the underworld and the trauma survivor fighting chaos.

The Lone Ranger Legend

The Lone Ranger was an exclusive product of American radio (Durning 1976). He was created as a character by George W. Trandle and fleshed out as a radio serial for children by the staff of WXYZ. After it was developed as a theme, "The Lone Ranger" was written into scripts by Fran Striker, who introduced silver as a prominent symbol. The first show aired January 30, 1933, and most of us who grew up in North America between then and now recognize the familiar story.

The Lone Ranger was one of six Texas Rangers who were ambushed by a gang of outlaws led by Butch Cavandish. The Rangers were betrayed by their scout. Dan Reid led the Rangers in their pursuit of the outlaws, and his brother, John, the sole survivor of the group, was wounded in the ambush and left for dead. John Reid was found by Tonto and nursed back to health in a cave, after remaining unconscious for three days. Tonto dug six graves to fool the outlaws into believing all six Rangers had died. The meeting was especially significant because John Reid had saved Tonto's life when they were boys.

After returning to consciousness three days later, John Reid declared to Tonto his intent to conceal his identity, including his name and appearance. He said he would don a mask and pursue not only Butch Cavandish but all the outlaws who roamed the West. Tonto would be his faithful friend, and they would travel together from crisis to crisis, fighting on the side of Good against Evil.

The radio announcer introduced the Lone Ranger as riding "on a fiery horse, with the speed of light, a cloud of dust. . . ." His horse's name was Silver. As a wild horse, Silver was legendary for his speed. The Lone Ranger searched for Silver because he was the only horse fast enough to catch Butch Cavandish. He found and rescued Silver when the horse was losing a battle with a giant buffalo. Silver remained wild and obeyed the Lone Ranger's commands only because he was grateful.

The wealth with which the Lone Ranger financed his adventures came from his secret silver mine. He had owned the mine with his brother and then his brother's son, Dan

Junior, who himself survived a wagon train massacre in which his mother was killed. The Lone Ranger had the silver molded into ammunition for his guns, and the silver bullet came to be his calling card. The dear cost of silver compelled him to use his weapons sparingly. It seems that after every big gunfight he had to return to his secret silver mine for a new supply of bullets.

No one who encountered the Lone Ranger knew his name. He was frequently mistaken for an outlaw. He furthered the confusion about his identity by being a master of disguise, especially when he needed to go among the townspeople to gather information. From my recall of the series, it seemed that his most frequent disguise was that of an old prospector.

The Survivor Syndrome

In the Lone Ranger theme, which seems to have sprung from a collective effort, we can see the symbolic representations of the survivor syndrome, with guilt and anger represented by the compulsive fighting, the mask and anonymity, the polarization of the world into good and evil, and the compulsive dedication never to forget, leading the Lone Ranger to swear to fight forever for justice (and perpetuate the trauma experience). Before the ambush, he was compelled to promise his brother that he would protect his brother's family, and Tonto and the Lone Ranger are also bound to each other by each having rescued the other from death.

Chief among the more subtle symptoms of survivor guilt is identity confusion. The survivor asks, in essence: "Part of me has died with the others, so who am I now?"—which addresses the life-altering magnitude of the trauma. The "others," of course, can be parts of one's identity that are crushed and repressed by the trauma.

The Lone Ranger is a master of disguises. There is a hermetic or trickster quality about the outlaw disguise, suggesting change, flux, or borderline behavior, depicted, as Jung pointed out, by quicksilver (1931). The Lone Ranger's predecessor, the Scarlet Pimpernel, was similarly adept at disguise when crossing borders. The Old West of the Lone Ranger was all borderland. In Homer's *Odyssey*, Odysseus returns home from war, after ten years of wandering, disguised by Athena as an old man in order to fool his enemies while observing them. In the legend of the Lone Ranger, loss of identity is further emphasized when Tonto symbolically buries John Reid with his dead comrades. Each episode seemed to end with the refrain, "Who was that masked man?"

Hermes, Mercury, Trickster, Raven, Coyote, Hare, Quicksilver, Mercurio are all denizens of the twilight border between consciousness and unconsciousness, between the sun god and the moon goddess. In modern culture, the characters are Batman, Superman, Zorro, the Green Hornet, etc. Their common motif is wealth, strength, secrecy, speed, energy, power, and mutability. Silver, in the context of the Lone Ranger legend, suggests energy. Silver, the horse, is a wild creature of tremendous speed, and it seems that the Lone Ranger can accomplish his goal of revenge only by harnessing Silver's wild energy, and only if Silver wishes to cooperate, suggesting that the energy is elusive to conscious direction. Money or wealth is a symbol for energy, and it is important that the Lone Ranger must go underground, suggesting a fundamental resource or unconscious depth, to get his secret wealth. (In Jack Benny's radio satire of the secret wealth motif, his underground vault is guarded by a Civil War veteran.)

One is immediately reminded of the motif of descent in myth, which Jung elucidated in his "On the Psychology of the Unconscious" (1943). The hero must go underground to find direction and renewal, or he descends into hell, only to rise again from the dead. Dionysus went into the underworld to retrieve his mother; Aeneas went into hell to find direction for himself and his Trojan survivors. There is a fairy-tale motif of the underground miners, who protect wealth and also watch over mankind, who are discovered through a near-death experience (see Lang 1966). Huck Finn, the wandering trickster of American folklore, has money which he found in a cave, kept in trust and representing to him boundless wealth.

As described earlier in chapter 1, recent trauma research by Kolb (1987), van der Kolk (1988a, 1988b, 1989), and others substantiates earlier observations that psychic trauma excites the brain and thus sends a tremendous charge to the entire nervous system. Survivors report adrenaline bursts that expand their awareness of potential and capacity. These newly discovered regions, unfortunately, are so associated with pain and fear that they tend not to be kept in consciousness and are repressed. Some survivors say that they have never felt as alive as when facing death. Hyperarousal and sudden change in mood thus become the characteristics of trauma memory and the trauma complex. The trauma imagery is never far away from consciousness and shares the power of the trauma's intensity. One war veteran reported a repeating dream of a Western desert cyclone, which was his image for the tropical hurricane as he experienced it hitting his coastal position in Vietnam. The experience of the dream is always terrifying. One thinks of Pan about to materialize from the swirl.

The memory of cataclysm, thinly veiled by repression, haunts the psyche like knowledge of the Apocalypse. The survivors often are so changed by trauma(s) that we describe them by their new survivor behavior; trauma symptoms dominate the personality. The phrase from the Lone Ranger's radio announcer is that "danger lies at the end of every trail," revealing the survivor's constant vigilance and apprehension that trauma will repeat. What the survivor experiences by the trauma arousal is what Krystal (1978, 1988) referred to as "overreactive affect," Pitman (1989) referred to as "super conditioning," and Wilson and Zigelbaum (1983) called "affective flooding." Psychodynamic theorists refer to this flux of energy as libido cathexis, and Jung wrote of it as canalization (1948a). This propensity of the survivor to react with energy fluxes causes the trauma complex to become associated with the merest hints of danger. Injustice, for instance, becomes a trigger for rage; the stress of the expressway becomes a battlefield; the sexual innuendo repeats a rape experience.

Silver is a repetitive symbol in the Lone Ranger. Silver has silver horseshoes. Like an unconscious source of energy, Silver is found in the wild and cannot be tamed. Jung (1944) explored the alchemists' use of quicksilver or mercury. The elusive homunculus demigod whom the alchemists called Mercurio is noted for the speed of his transformations. Mercurio in alchemy is the shadowy doorman of the unconscious, passing in and out of consciousness, changing shape and identity. The alchemists saw Mercurio as both residing in the base substance of nature and capable of transforming into gold. To make the transformation, the alchemists added salt to mercury. With the bitter salt of experience, the base substance was transformed. Salt is the precursor of Luna. From Luna comes the sun (Jung 1944). These are the shadow figures that are activated by the infusion of traumatic energy and continue to influence behavior after trauma.

The Sun Heroes

The precursors of the Lone Ranger legend are a succession of wandering sun heroes in the mythology of Western cultures: Theseus, Aeneas, Jason, Christ, Ulysses, Galahad, etc., as well as Cu Chullain of the Celts, and Raven of the Haida, Kwakiutl, Bella Coola, and other northwest coast natives. Modern cinema depictions of sun heroes are numerous. As mentioned in the introduction, Ingmar Bergman (1960) recently recreated a sun hero returning from the war and stalked by Death in his film, *The Seventh Seal.*

One remarkable characteristic of these more modern heroes is the presence of a second figure, a servant or companion, who is a complement to the hero in personality and style. Often this figure is the one who gets things done. The hero and his shadow figure are the result of a traumatic division of consciousness. Prior to the trauma event, consciousness had been more unified in relation to its own unconscious. In the Lone Ranger legend, John Reid is traumatized, Tonto appears on the battlefield, and the survivor is transformed into a masked man; John Reid has been split into the Lone Ranger and Tonto. Tonto is in touch with the wilderness and knows the lore of the land. He is the source of information about primitive wisdom and survival, and he is the one who can go anonymously among various peoples to gather the latest news. He alone knows the Lone Ranger's true identity.

I use the term *hero* here after Jung, who wrote:

> What we seek in visible human form is not man, but the superman, the hero, or god, that quasi-human being who symbolizes the ideas, forms, and forces which grip and mould the soul. (1956, par. 259).

For the trauma survivor, the quest for wholeness, which was fragmented by trauma and repression, is the hero's quest. Gender has nothing to do with trauma *per se,* and the dynamics of trauma recovery are not affected by the sex so much as by the style of the survivor. The same myths apply. When identity is repressed, it is forced into the unconscious and buried there. One hears the expressions: "I died in Vietnam." "Part of me died when I was raped." Such expressions describe the radical change imposed on the survivor by psychic trauma. What gets buried is energy representing significant images and emotions relating to the trauma experience. An exception to this might be the single-event trauma to a child (Terr 1990a), although repeating trauma would produce the numbing and denial symptomatic of psychic death. This energy lost to ego's command is not lost to the whole being, although the survivor may feel suddenly aged because the survivor's ego has lost part of its energy. Symbolically expressed, the hero has split into the survivor and his or her shadow, and the shadow has become personified. In the first radio show of "The Lone Ranger," Tonto's appearance is noted with religious hush befitting the emergence of a god from the underworld. As we shall see, the repressed energy can merge with habits and take on a new life in the survivor.

Strength of Habit and the Autonomous Complex

Survivors of trauma are prone to develop secondary habits which initially help the survivor cope with the trauma disorder and which in turn become associated with the energy of the trauma complex. It is these habits that tap and use the complex's energy. They may be habits that numb the trauma pain, distract and entertain the ego, or direct attention away from the complex. As habits are prone to do, they gain strength through repetition, forming worn trails in the brain. Essentially, coping habits form around the two currently recognized classes of PTSD symptoms: avoidance and repetition.

The learning theorist Clark Hull (Hilgard and Bower 1966) examined the function of what he called "habit strength" in the shaping of behavior. Hull influenced other theorists, who have since elaborated on the basic learning concept that habits grow strong and are maintained through reinforcement and repetition, and that habitual activity may become self-reinforcing, i.e., the act becomes its own reward or, to paraphrase Marshall McLuhan's famous phrase, the medium becomes the message.

Jung (1948a), in his discussion of the autonomous complex, allowed for the existence and maintenance of habits. Habits constellate their own energy by manifesting periodically in behavior, thereby forming an autonomous habit complex. Those who are in prolonged or repeated states of emergency, such as soldiers in prolonged combat, develop habitual ways of coping with trauma emotions. These coping methods are effective at first. They become, as it were, reliable friends to aid in relief from the war. For example, when whiskey was introduced to the troops of the Civil War, it was used as anesthesia. After that war, addiction to whiskey became known as "the Army disease" (Wecter 1944); a habit that had developed in coping with traumatic stress became named for the stressor. Other modern wars developed their characteristic addictions. British officers in the trenches during the First World War had unlimited access to whiskey. Robert Graves (1951) refers to the problem of "dipsomania" causing the British officers to commit gross mistakes in battle. In Korea, there was a popular toxic drink among the Americans called GI gin. In Vietnam, marijuana and opium vied with alcohol for popularity.

Children who are repeatedly traumatized develop behavior disorders of withdrawal or hyperactivity. Old habits are renewed that provide security. Abused children become addicted to their own emergency endorphin release (van der Kolk 1989). Addictions to street drugs typically develop in adolescence. The legalistic terms *truancy* or *runaway* are often indicative of trauma avoidance symptoms. The behavior that works in coping with the traumatic stress becomes habit when the stress is prolonged, and eventually becomes the partner of the ego in assisting its survival. The ego and the habit, like the Lone Ranger and Tonto, save each other time after time in a world where danger lies at the end of every trail. The ego maintains the habit, and the habit protects the ego.

In the first Lone Ranger episode on radio, when Tonto and John Reid recognize each other from childhood, we learn that Tonto as a child had referred to his rescuer as Kemo Sabe, a phrase that means "faithful friend." Tonto, in effect, is the split-off energy representative of the repressed psyche, the personal unconscious of the hero, personified by the infusion of energy, with access to the collective tradition of the unconscious. Habits similarly become faithful friends, sources of knowledge and wealth, and reliable refuges from pain and ennui. Eating habits become to some survivors what drug and alcohol habits and gambling are to others.

The hero and the helpful shadow can be seen in a wide range of literature from children's comics, such as Batman and Robin, to the European legends of the king and his jester. This motif is satirized in Don Quixote and Sancho Panza, the radio serial of "The Cisco Kid" and Pancho, and even in Dashiell Hammett's "Thin Man" series. From an earlier era, as we shall review in chapter 5, Robert Louis Stevenson's *The Strange Case of Dr. Jekyll and Mr. Hyde* represents an ego and habit/trauma complex combination that remains unintegrated and does not work.

Clinical experience has shown that one can approach habit problems through trauma or trauma problems through the treatment of habits. Those who are traumatized at a young age produce habits that become styles that, in turn, produce personality disorders. Those who treat habits and addictions should not ignore trauma in the patient, any more than the analyst can ignore the habit.

Summary

The radio staff who produced "The Lone Ranger" probably had no awareness that they were writing an accurate portrayal of the survivor syndrome. They were in competition with other stations and wanted to write a popular kids' show. That they stepped into their archetypal river is no surprise, Jung would say, because the collective psyche is deeper and wider (while it is at the same time narrower and more shallow) than the individuals who compose it. One man had an idea and others responded with their own imaginations, and when we hear the horns in the opening bars of the *William Tell Overture,* even today, our memories of The Lone Ranger are constellated in us and we smile.

"The Lone Ranger" is derived from the same sources of Celtic legend that produced the Arthurian legends. In the next chapter, "Sir Gawain and the Green Knight" is used to explore the problems of sleep disturbance and fear of madness that the survivor must face after a near-death experience.

Chapter

4

THE PERILOUS BED

Sir Gawain and the Near-Death Experience

"Remarkable things happen when warriors clash, and emotions of the passionately aroused temper are remarkable. Where is the line of demarcation between the natural and the miraculous?"

Walter Otto, *The Homeric Gods*

Psychic trauma often occurs as the result of what is perceived by the survivor as a near-death experience. Recently van der Kolk (1989) described the physiology of the tendency to repeat the traumatic experience. As discussed in previous chapters, behaviors similar to the compulsion to repeat trauma are found in mythology, legend, and folk tales which give us very old pictures of attempts at healing trauma disorder in which the protagonist is brought near death and undertakes trials of enchantment and wandering to seek the treasure of renewal. In Arthurian legend, the knight Gawain is one of those who undertakes such a quest by pitting himself against an overwhelming foe.

"Sir Gawain and the Green Knight" is perhaps the best expression of this mythical motif, which is generally considered to be Celtic in origin (Sjoestedt 1982; Zimmer 1971). Other versions can be found in *Bullfinch's Mythology* and the

Welsh Mabinogion (Gantz 1976). In the fourteenth-century version of the motif (Stone 1982), a giant in green appears before the assemblage of knights at King Arthur's court. In his fine regalia, he appears to be a nobleman from an earlier age. He is fearsome, toting a battle ax of enormous size and a sprig of holly. He wears no armor. His age and antiquity suggest a vegetation deity, the holly suggests the winter saturnalia, and the whole effect suggests death. In earlier versions, the knight appears in black. In "Caradoc Briefbras" (*Bullfinch's Mythology*) he is the father/enchanter who appears on the occasion of Caradoc's initiation into the Round Table of Arthur's court.

The Green Knight challenges the court's honor and asks for a knight to meet him in contest. The contest the Green Knight proposes is for someone to cut his head off, someone who must in turn offer his own head to be cut off by the same knight a year later. So fearsome was the Green Knight that no one immediately took up the challenge. When Arthur, himself, moved to take the challenge, Gawain interceded and begged to be allowed to defend Arthur's honor.

> Before all, King, confide
> This fight to me. May it be mine.
> (Stone 1982, p. 33)

Gawain then cut off the giant's head, but the Green Knight was barely staggered by the blow. Instead, he picked up his head by his long green hair, leapt onto his horse, and reminded Gawain to appear in a year at the Green Chapel.

In a precursor to this fourteenth-century story, the gathering is of the heroes of the Irish Red Branch (Zimmer 1971). Here the giant Cu Roi appeared dressed in a garment of the Dagda, a more primitive deity. Cu Roi challenged the honor of the heroes by calling up the so-called "truth of men." He set the challenge for any hero to strike a blow and have the same blow received the next day. Three heroes, one after the other each day, rose to strike the blow, but then they each failed to return the next day. Each time Cu Roi returned with his head restored. Then the tribal hero, Cu Chulainn (literally "Dog of Chulainn"), took the challenge, thoroughly smashing Cu Roi's head. Cu Roi, however, returned unabashed and, as the true Celtic hero, Cu Chulainn submitted to his fate.

In all the versions, the hero defends the king by having a contest with death. However, the contest is unequal: death is a spirit, and the hero is then fated to submit to his own death. What is important is that the hero accepts his fate. "What should a man do but dare?" (Stone 1982, p. 42).

Having a sense that life is fated is a symptom of trauma disorder that can be passed on from generation to generation. Henry Krystal, looking at similar survivors, writes:

> In studies of traumatized people we must look for their defenses and reactions, and must specifically identify their *fate* before we can evaluate the after effects. (1967, p. 87, my emphasis)

Sixty percent of the combat veterans of the Vietnam War had fathers who had fought in World War II. The sons of veterans feel compelled to act in defense of the tradition. Homer described the passing on of the warrior's fate in the *Odyssey*:

> "My son, now we have come to the place of battle, where the best men are proved: you will know how not to disgrace your fathers, since our line has been notable over all the earth for courage and valor!"
>
> Telemachos answered: "You shall see, if you will my dear father, that my spirit shall bring no disgrace upon your line."
>
> Laertes was full of joy, and cried out: "What a day is this, kind gods! I am a happy man. My son and my son's son are rivals in courage!" (1937, p. 48)

How the hero goes to meet his fate is subject to much variation. Sir Gawain travels in search of the Green Knight's chapel much as other Arthurian knights went in search of the grail, not knowing where it was, traveling through wretched conditions, battling monsters, and meeting fearsome strangers and the wiles of enchanters. (In a process similar to wandering, Caradoc is affixed with a snake by the evil enchantress. The snake leeches his energy and he suffers.) The poet describes Gawain's troubled search:

He faltered not nor feared,
But quickly went his way
His road was rough and weird,
Or so the stories say.
. . . .
His way was wild and strange
By dreary hill and dean.
His mood would many times change
Before that fane was seen.
(Stone 1982, pp. 47–48)

What is important about the interim phase of the wandering in Gawain's saga is the absence of any knowledge of direction. There is no sense of having a trail or path. Gawain's so-called "gruesome quest," with its suffering and isolation, is indicative of the hero's quest. He wanders about subject to the whimsical cruelty of nature. He must ask strangers to direct him through their lands. He fights battles with dangerous men who are fierce giants in stature. The monsters he meets are of mythical prowess. Since he has no way to go, he drops his reins and lets nature and chance decide.

The hero in this quest enters the dark territory of the moon goddess, represented in Gawain's story by Morgan le Fay. It is finally revealed in the poem that Morgan has launched an attack on the perfect lady, Arthur's Guinevere, by sending the Green Knight to Arthur's court, hoping that the sight of him would scare sweet Guinevere to death.

It is worth noting here that the Arthur of this story was a mythical character taken up in the oral tradition, much as Robin Hood was later made mythical. The historical Arthur was a general at the time the Roman legions retreated from Britain. He led the Britons' struggle against the Saxon armies that Rome had kept at bay. There is a sense that Arthur, as he became a myth, came to represent and defend the new patriarchal order, established through the Romanization of the Celts. By the standards of Roman chroniclers, the Celts had been remarkable for their fierce warriors who battled without armor, often charging naked at the Roman legions. The ideals of knightly honor and courtly love came later, a result of the discipline that was required to keep the Romanized civilization (which I think of as the patriarchal order) intact, a discipline which advocated passion in restraint.

The quest aspect of Gawain's saga is very reminiscent of the trauma survivor's frustrating quest to recover from trauma disorder, which is the death challenge. That quest, with its isolation, alienation, bouts of depression and anger, is largely directed inward in the form of guilt, self-criticism, and self-defeating behaviors. Bettelheim (1979, p. 28) found that among concentration camp survivors, one way to deal with the traumas was to engage in a lifelong struggle to remain aware and try to cope.

Trauma survivors often have an altered perception of time. Trauma tends to bisect the survivor's life into before and after, with the time of the trauma magnified vividly. Survivors are prone to develop a sense of futurelessness such that they fail to anticipate problems that come from their own actions. They fight wars with institutions, which have become the mythical beasts of the twentieth century.

The Green Knight's Test

Gawain finally arrives at a castle which turns out to belong to the Green Knight disguised as a gentleman, who proposes a whimsical contest. The gentleman, the lord of the castle, will go out hunting and bring all his day's catch to Gawain, and Gawain must in turn give all he has gained that day in exchange. This contest goes on for three days. Each night, while Gawain sleeps, the beautiful lady of the castle enters his chamber and flirts with him.

To be tested in bed implies problems with both sexual intimacy and sleep disturbance, both remarkable symptoms of PTSD. One of the Irish goddesses of the matriarchal era was the Morrigan, Queen of Demons. She would lie on the chests of her warrior victims and give them nightmares. Her sisters were Badb, the Raven of Battle, and Nemain, whose name meant Panic (Sjoestedt 1982). Others (Graves 1948) refer to Madb as one of the goddesses of war. In other stories of the Arthurian cycle (Zimmer 1971), *Perceval*, for example, the knight is forewarned and goes to bed with his armor on. The bed attacks him, bucking like a wild horse.

Being tested in bed is a common experience of the trauma survivor. The perilous bed of the trauma survivor is one of sleep disturbance, which begins as arousal from the midbrain and proceeds to activate the cortex, manifesting in the form of intrusive and compulsive thoughts of trauma, surges of emotional arousal, anxiety and anger, night terrors, nightmares, and night sweats. *Nightmare* is a German word referring to the witch who comes in dreams. Sex with the dark moon goddess represents madness to the surviving warriors of many mythologies. Circe is Odysseus's nightmare in Homer's *Odyssey.*

The lady of the castle slips into Gawain's bedroom while the castle is deserted by the lord on his hunt.

> She came by the chamber door and closed it after her
> Cast open a casement and called on the knight,
> And briskly thus rebuked him with bountiful words of
> good cheer
> "Ah sir! What, sound asleep?"
> (Stone 1982, p. 86)

She is dressed for seduction, and she loquaciously offers herself to the knight. Gawain's task is not only to refuse her without offending her, but, at the same time, to flatter her and offer himself to her service. This he does elegantly, and they chatter in a courtly manner. She kisses him, and when Gawain meets his host next morning (who is indeed the Green Knight), he must give him the kiss in exchange for the bounty of the lord's hunt, which is a number of slain harts. The scene is repeated the next day, and she gives Gawain two kisses, which he gives to the lord in exchange for the corpse of a wild boar. The hart and the boar are sacred to Diana/Artemis. The boar was a commonly used medieval symbol for wild natural instinct.

The following day the lady appears with her breasts exposed and directly offers herself to Gawain, who, in turn, again deftly offers to honor her while declining her sexual favors. She kisses him three times and proposes an exchange of gifts. Gawain has nothing to give her. She at first offers him her ring. He declines the ring but accepts instead her lace girdle. It is unclear if he accepts the girdle to balance the honor he declares is her due, or if he really covets the girdle because it is charmed with the power to protect its wearer from death.

When the lord of the castle returns on the third evening, he has killed a varmint fox, which he presents to Gawain in exchange for Gawain's three kisses. The fox is a universal symbol of the "shape-shifter" or trickster. Gawain hides the girdle, and the next morning he rides off to the Green Chapel to meet the fearsome knight.

Knightly Honor

Knightly honor protects against the primitive emotions that produce destructive violence. When Cu Chulainn visits the dwelling of Scathach (the Shadowy One) and is greeted by his daughter, Uathach (the Terrible), the hero assaults her and, with violent force, he overcomes her (Sjoestedt 1982). In these earlier versions of the Gawain theme, it is the ability to conjure sudden violent fury that is heroic. Without the code of knightly honor, the fearsomeness of Cu Chulainn is displayed in his physical distortions and his ability to demolish his enemies unremittingly. The development of knightly honor, to the knights of Gawain's time, represents the equivalent of discipline to the modern trauma survivor, which leads to the development of will to be steadfast before the Maiden of Madness, the nightmare.

In our fourteenth-century version, knightly honor prevents Gawain from engaging his passion with the lady, even in the face of her most tempting advances. The slain beasts are a clue to the source of the Green Knight's power. He is an agent for the dark moon goddess, Artemis. Gawain does not realize that by refusing the lady in such tempting circumstances, he is saving himself from annihilation.

The trauma survivor seeks to isolate himself or herself from tempting passions, emotions of all sorts, which might unlock the terror and pain of the trauma. The rules of conduct in this version of courtly love and knightly honor are similar to behavior that the trauma survivor must follow before reentering society. After one has experienced the threat of death by being overwhelmed and acquired knowledge of the brutality of nature (including the witnessing of one's own primitive arousal), one is cut off from society. The survivor is preoccupied with controlling his or her own responses. This is at first facilitated by the traumatic activation of the endogenous opioidal system promoting psychic numbing and dissociation. Later avoidant behavior includes anxiety, anger, and worry, leading to social isolation, habitual intoxication, compulsive work or travel, and emotional detachment.

> He was less love-laden because of the loss he must now face
> His destruction by the stroke,
> for come it must was the case.
> (Stone 1982, p. 89)

One World War II veteran described the struggle for readjustment this way:

> It may sound like exaggeration, but I actually feel like a stranger in my own home, because every day living in America requires emotional responses which I am incapable of giving. (Waller 1944)

Knightly honor requires the knight to be perfect in his conduct, controlling his passions and showing compassion for the less fortunate and mercy to those he defeats (providing they profess a similar code). The time of Arthur represents a precarious time when barbarism and the return of matriarchy are seen as threatening nature (dragons, monsters, etc.). The threat required a dedication to perfection in order to survive. Dedication to discipline built ego strength and the smallest flaw produced shame.

> He groaned at his disgrace,
> Unfolding his ill-fame,
> And blood suffused his face
> When he showed his mark of shame.
> (Stone 1982, p. 114)

The shame referred to is Gawain's for being caught not turning over the girdle. He feels caught "by cowardice and covetousness." The poet says that he thereafter wore the girdle on his arm as a badge of shame and observes that the knights of Arthur's court thereafter wore a green garter on their arms as a tribute to Gawain.

There is a similar encounter when combat veterans meet. When medals for valor are known, the paradox is that the higher the honor, the greater the shame of the wearer and the greater the respect from fellow combatants, who yet understand the shame that death produces. Nor, in contrast, is any conduct considered more cowardly than that of the man or woman who wears a medal for valor he or she does not deserve but has acquired through vainglorious ambition. (In later chapters, the problem of shame and humiliation in the trauma survivor will be discussed in more detail.)

Gawain is thus a parable of the trauma survivor. When he goes to meet his fate at the Green Knight's chapel, he is met by the knight rudely sharpening his ax. Gawain puts his head on the block and is nicked by the knight on the neck. The wound is a token punishment for his dishonesty in not giving the lord his due—the lady's gift of the green girdle. The Green Knight then tells Gawain that he is a gentleman who has been enchanted by Morgan le Fay, whose intent it was to frighten her sister, Arthur's Queen Guinevere, to death.

The theme is repeated in other stories of unwanted consciousness resulting from trauma. Psychological trauma causes exposure to the dark side of the goddess.

> So "Morgan the Goddess"
> She accordingly became;
> The proudest she can oppress
> And to her purpose tame—
> (Stone 1982, p. 112)

If there is trauma in the threat of death, that is certainly what Gawain encounters. He is fated, his future foreshortened. He is cast into isolation, pain, and desolate wandering in his quest to repeat the encounter with death. He is tested in bed by the moon goddess and regaled with the bounty of nature. He responds with courage and clever deception. Gawain is similar to the Grimms' (1972) discharged soldier in "Bearskin," noted in chapter 2, who enters a pact with the chthonic divinity, in which he is tested with misery, before he can be returned to wholeness.

The dark side of the goddess—Artemis, Morgan le Fay, the Morrigan—represents nature in the raw. She possesses and hounds the survivor by exposure to trauma once he or she has witnessed her. A remnant of this fear of the goddess can be found as late as Mark Twain's Huck Finn, who describes the bad luck that is got from looking at the new moon accidentally, "that way, like a fool" (Twain 1980, p. 676).

The moon goddess captures the proud and the dutiful who would fight for the king. Her tests, like the tests of the devil in the Grimms' tale, provide both trial and wealth simultaneously. Within the experience of psychological trauma there is energy that enables the survivor to reach wholeness and a richness of higher consciousness that would not have been possible without having had the test.

Summary

In the various versions of "Sir Gawain and the Green Knight," the hero is tested by a god of another age, his father, who is enchanted by a dark goddess. To succeed at the test, he must do the impossible and endure suffering. He cannot succeed without the assistance of a beautiful woman, whom he must love spiritually. She represents the energy of the dark goddess that has been excited by the experience of trauma. She represents both the threat of madness and the hope of recovery. The hero of these tales is like the survivor of psychic trauma who cannot avoid the symptoms of PTSD, its suffering, wandering, and visits from the dark goddess, but who can only go into them and endure them and prevail by using the wild energy generated by the trauma to integrate the new consciousness exposed by the trauma.

The next chapter is a case study of sorts, in which the nightmare of repeating psychological trauma is defended against by separating the trauma complex from the ego.

Chapter

5

ROBERT LOUIS STEVENSON'S NIGHTMARE

The Case of Dr. Jekyll and Mr. Hyde

Psychological trauma puts the psyche at odds with itself by injecting unwanted emotions and images into consciousness. The psychic content of trauma becomes a threat that must be coped with by whatever means are available: dissociation, distraction, intoxication, denial, or projection. "The Strange Case of Dr. Jekyll and Mr. Hyde" describes the problem Robert Louis Stevenson had in coping with repeated psychological trauma. Stevenson was a survivor of what I have classified as "natural trauma," a repeating childhood near-death trauma caused by his chronic respiratory illness. His trauma complex showed up in his nightmare and from his nightmare he wrote the story.

In our culture, the phrase "Jekyll and Hyde" is used to describe someone who radically changes personality from good to bad. A 1982 Seattle newspaper carried this headline on an article about alcoholism: "Cocktail hour turns this Jekyll into Hyde," although there was no other reference to Robert Louis Stevenson's story.

I have heard veterans who were traumatized by war, as well as adults who were repeatedly abused as children, refer to shadow monsters in their minds virtually identical to Hyde: an uncivilized, violently angry and vengeful, traumatized beast or witch that remained yet unintegrated. Stevenson, like Mary Shelley, Bram Stoker, and others of his time, managed to capture in writing the archetypal monster who represented trauma in the psyche of the author. In Stevenson's well-documented life, the traumatic effects of his prolonged respiratory illness are clearly illustrated. Stevenson struggled to suppress his energy because overactivity exacerbated his illness. It is his own nightmare that is described in the story of Dr. Jekyll and Mr. Hyde, and its popularity suggests that it also reflected a collective nightmare of Stevenson's time, as well as perhaps our own.

The Strange Case

"The Strange Case of Dr. Jekyll and Mr. Hyde" reads like a good mystery thriller. A gentleman lawyer, Mr. Utterson, is told by a friend, Mr. Enfield, about an encounter with the nasty Edward Hyde. Enfield witnessed Hyde trampling a child and then participated in a group of citizens that confronted Hyde, who was fined on the spot. Part of the fine was paid with a check signed by the famous humanitarian, Dr. Henry Jekyll. Utterson was aware that Jekyll, who coincidentally was Utterson's client, had recently revised his will to leave his possessions to none other than Edward Hyde, the monstrous man who had trampled the child. Disturbed by this, Utterson visited a mutual friend, a prestigious doctor named Lanyon. He learned that Lanyon and Jekyll were no longer close because of Jekyll's unorthodox chemical experiments. Utterson's curiosity was piqued, and he searched out and finally encountered Hyde himself. He then visited Jekyll's home but only talked to the servant, Poole, and learned that Hyde was a frequent visitor whom the servants were ordered to obey. Two weeks later, still concerned, he visited Jekyll and offered to help, being convinced that Hyde was blackmailing Jekyll. Jekyll, however, exhibited unconcern. Then, on one of his nighttime escapades, Hyde murdered a prominent citizen (another of Utterson's clients), and although he was identified by a witness, he managed to disappear. Utterson visited Jekyll again and found the latter shaken over news of the murder, but insistent that he would never see Hyde again.

After some time passed, Utterson was invited to visit Lanyon, who was said to be dying from a terrible shock he had received. Utterson learned later that the shock was not from seeing Hyde, but, ironically, from witnessing Hyde turn into Jekyll. Still not connecting the two as one, Utterson repeatedly attempted to talk to Jekyll but was refused an audience. Lanyon finally died and left Utterson a letter to be opened upon Jekyll's death. After more time had passed, Utterson was suddenly summoned to Jekyll's house by a worried Poole, who believed the reclusive Jekyll had met with foul play. Together they broke into Jekyll's laboratory and found Hyde within, dead, and Jekyll nowhere to be found. Utterson read Lanyon's letter and we learn what we may have suspected—that Jekyll was Hyde. Utterson then read Jekyll's letter, which chronicled the story of how Jekyll sought to separate physically his hedonistic side from his "good" side by ingesting a chemical concoction. Jekyll described how Hyde gradually grew in energy and power, how the chemical compound was flawed and could not be replicated, how Hyde gradually took over (manifested involuntarily), and how he finally ran out of the compound that transformed him back into Jekyll, forcing him to conceal himself and finally to commit suicide.

I am reminded of Oscar Wilde's lament in "De Profundis": "one had either to give up to you or to give you up." In his letter from prison to his lover, Wilde wrote:

> I had made a gigantic psychological error. I had always thought that my giving up to you in small things meant nothing: that when a great moment arrived I could myself reassert my willpower in its natural superiority. It was not so. At the great moment my willpower completely failed me. (Wilde 1982, p. 104)

Stevenson and His Times

All of Robert Louis Stevenson's biographers (Daiches 1973, Hennessy 1974, Calder 1980) agree that he came to write "The

Strange Case of Dr. Jekyll and Mr. Hyde" by first dreaming it in a nightmare. He is said to have been awakened by his wife, Fanny, and to have been angry because he was interrupted in his dreaming. He was accustomed to taking material from his dreams (he was always looking for horror or suspense stories), and he wrote this story in three days. Stevenson burned the story after a discussion with Fanny and, in three more days, wrote another version, the one we have today.

Stevenson had a severe respiratory problem all his life. He was forced to spend much of his time in bed and was given to hemorrhaging when he overexerted himself, yet he had at the same time an abundance of energy. In his youth, his parents and childhood nurse read him adventure stories and recounted Scottish tales to help pass his time in bed. Stevenson's father had an adventurous spirit, too, and later expressed pleasure at his son's adventure stories. Robert Louis's imagination was expanded by the storytelling combined with his illness that forced him into inactivity, giving him a propensity for fantasy.

Mary Shelley similarly reports a common penchant for fantasy resulting from repeated mother loss (her mother at birth, then her surrogate mother at age three): "her desperate desire for a loving and supportive parent defined her character, shaped her fantasies, and produced her fictional idealizations" (Mellor 1988, p. 1). Her novel, *Frankenstein*, was also created from a nightmare endured during the stormy, dark, eerie summer following the eruption of the Tamporo volcano (Sigurdsson and Carey 1988).

Terr (1987) gives us a touching account of the psychological trauma in the mistreatment of Edith Wharton's typhoid. Wharton, a contemporary of Stevenson, subsequently "played out" her trauma complex in her writing.

That childhood illness or medical procedures can become traumatic was discussed in chapter 1. The critical ingredient of trauma is the overwhelming of the ego identity without preparation, creating a primitive, instinctual awareness that experiences the hyperarousal of the trauma as a threat of extinction. This hyperarousal, utilizing inherent capacity, later reactivates on cue, causing panic, which in turn may lead to habitual chronic arousal. For example, a child who at age five has open-heart surgery requiring her ribs to be broken experiences her parents as abandoning her in the hospital; later, as an adult, she experiences violent, morbid, bloody fantasies and develops a taste for ghastly true-crime stories.

In all likelihood, Stevenson eventually developed a dependency on opiated medications administered to treat his illness. He appears to have utilized his activated fantasy to process his trauma into stories. He loved to write what he called "crawlers," mysteries with a horror twist. Writing was not the Stevenson family trade, however; three generations of men on Stevenson's father's side were lighthouse engineers, and his father achieved recognition and prosperity in his profession. Robert Louis significantly wrote "The Strange Case of Dr. Jekyll and Mr. Hyde" while living in a home named for the most famous Stevenson deep-sea lighthouse (famous for shining light into dark places). Stevenson's love of adventure, as seen in his novels *Kidnapped* and *Treasure Island,* sustained his romantic spirit throughout his life; yet because he was frail, energetic activity was life-threatening. While in college in Edinburgh, he enjoyed relatively good health and was very active, but he also had to allow for long periods of recovery after bouts of overactivity. During one spell of activity, he visited the United States and married Fanny. It was also on that visit that he had a near-death experience caused by his illness and was rescued while hiking in the hills of California and nursed back to health in a mountain cabin. Fanny worried about his health and thought that his enthusiastic college friends drained him of his energy. Stevenson himself regarded life and the world as brutal. According to Hennessy's biography, Stevenson wrote in a letter:

> . . . a child should early gain some perception of what the world is really like—its baseness, its treacheries, its thinly veneered brutalities. (1974, p. 170)

Stevenson seems in many ways remarkably adjusted to his illnesses. He continued to work in bed the way he had played in bed as an invalid child and regarded his infirmities as an accident of nature. Yet, he must have been frustrated at the confinement. Calder gives this picture of him:

> Louis in conversation rarely stayed in the same place for long. When he was not actually reduced to his bed or at his desk writing, he was in motion, incessantly smoking, pacing and prowling the room that caged him. (1980, p. 90)

Stevenson was a medical case all his life. He was ferried from doctor to doctor, and nobody was able to cure him. He must have wondered whether medicine knew what it was about, and his often weak and drugged condition must have sapped his confidence. It seems that only Fanny was a true guide and comfort, protecting him and lending him strength.

At the time he was writing "Dr. Jekyll and Mr. Hyde" in 1885, Stevenson's life was in a difficult time of transition. A close friend was dying of alcoholism. His own father was dying, and did indeed die shortly after the story was published. His own constant illness kept him bedridden and became worse after his return to England from a Swiss sanitarium. He was hemorrhaging and often so weak that Fanny had to carry him when it was necessary to move him. The description of Henry Jekyll could well be of Stevenson himself:

> I became, in my own person, a creature eaten up and emptied by fever, languidly weak both in body and mind, and solely occupied by one thought: the horror of my other self. (Stevenson 1979, p. 95)

Stevenson was writing and also receiving numerous visitors, and these activities drained him. He may well have been addicted to drugs by this time; the three most frequently used in those days for the treatment of fever were laudanum, morphine, and opium—all addictive opiates. We know from Fanny's diary that in his college days he displayed highly labile emotions, throwing himself on the ground weeping or having fits of uncontrollable laughter, behaviors that reflect drug toxicity or withdrawal symptoms. If Stevenson was addicted to opiates, it was probably to avoid pain rather than induce pleasure. Stevenson had a nineteenth-century Scottish Calvinist cultural heritage that regarded virtually any pleasurable indulgence as excessive. "It is the Calvinist view," writes Calder in her biography, "that man must maintain a constant struggle with evil, that the slightest lapse in vigilance will allow the Devil to triumph" (1980, p. 221). Although Stevenson, as an adult, was agnostic, he is not likely to have used his medicine for self-indulgence.

The Construction of Jekyll and Hyde

Stevenson's device for unfolding his nightmarish story is the detectivelike work of the taciturn Utterson. This is effective dramatically, creating a mystery that is not fully revealed until the last lines, and it also removes the reader from direct involvement in the horror. Even Utterson gets all the action secondhand. He has only one rather civil exchange with Hyde and two brief moments in direct contact with Jekyll through the course of the entire story.

What we know about Utterson is that he is solid and rugged but embarrassed in discourse and backward in sentiment, certainly a minimal personality, perhaps like Stevenson's father, there to further the story like a Dashiell Hammett gumshoe, a parsimonious observer and reporter. He is the protagonist and the fulcrum of the story. Significantly, he is described as "the last reputable acquaintance and the last influence in the lives of down-going men" (Stevenson 1979, p. 29).

In the remarkable opening scene, Utterson is walking with Enfield, an equally taciturn distant kinsman. Enfield is very like Utterson, except that he is a "well known man about town." Enfield appears to be the darker, more colorful side of Utterson, and therefore able to access information unavailable to the lawyer. In the course of their walk together, they come upon a "certain sinister block of building," and Enfield remarks on the door, which "bore in every feature the marks of prolonged and sordid negligence" (Stevenson 1979, p. 30). He then proceeds to tell Utterson of his late-night encounter with Hyde. Here I think we have an almost pure dream fragment, in the passage that begins, "I was coming from some place at the end of the world about three o'clock of a black winter morning . . ." (ibid., p. 31). In this scene (which in its physical description reminds me of the stylized scenes of early German cinema), Hyde tramples an eight-year-old girl with whom he has accidentally collided. The girl has been running to fetch a doctor. Hyde continues on and is collared by Enfield, and money is exacted from him to compensate the child's family. Hyde turns over ten pounds in gold and ninety pounds in a check signed by Jekyll. Enfield is aided in this by a doctor, who is described as your "usual cut-and-dry apothecary, of no particular age and color, with a strong Edinburgh accent, and about as emotional as a bagpipe" (ibid.). One wonders how many similar doctors Stevenson encountered in his youth.

If exacting money can be said to be symbolic of repression, it is interesting to note that Jekyll later sets up a separate bank account for Hyde as a result of this encounter, which further aids Hyde's autonomy and contributes to his recklessness. Indeed, through the course of the story there is a stream of energy that runs from Jekyll to Hyde. In the sequence discussed above, the price for Hyde's brutal insensitivity is paid one-tenth by Hyde and nine-tenths by Jekyll. The police inspector says later: "Money's life to the man" (ibid., p. 50). In Jekyll's letter at the end of the story, he says that his life has been "nine-tenths a life of effort, virtue and control." Hyde, he writes, "had been much less exercised and much less exhausted" (ibid., p. 84).

Hyde, as autonomous trauma complex to Jekyll's ego complex, actually acquires will as he takes over more and more conscious Jekyll energy. In his letter, Jekyll describes his involuntary transformation into Hyde in the public park. Heretofore, he had been able to control Hyde's appearances. Yet, once out, Hyde (paradoxically in the context of his attributes) has the strength of discipline to retire as discreetly as possible to a hotel to write his letters seeking help from Lanyon.

Jung describes this involuntary autonomous flow of complex energy as a "canalization of energy" (1948a, par. 79). It is similar to the intrusive recollection of trauma associations and the dissociative involuntary flashback, which are more likely to occur to a mind at rest or otherwise depleted of energy.

When we compare Jekyll to Hyde, the disparity of energy is dramatic. The following list of attributes is comprised of the adjectives used in the story, and thus are not one-to-one oppositions.

Jekyll's Characteristics	*Hyde's Characteristics*
spiritual	astute, impatient
a little drowsy	lusting, bold
a tall, fine man	apelike, angry
handsome	capable of will
one who does good	contemptuous of danger
known for religion and charities	faculties sharpened
open and bright	animal licking his chops
sad	inhuman child of hell
heretic	raging energies of life
penitent	wonderful love of life
	skulking, foul

In terms of the balance of power, Jekyll appears as a weakling compared to the robust Hyde. It is, after all, Hyde's zestful energy that attracts Jekyll, who "concealed his pleasures." Jekyll, in his letter to Lanyon, takes all the blame. He doesn't even suggest that it was a simple mistake, but rather, inherent in his ambitious imbalance:

> It was rather the exacting nature of my aspirations, than any particular degradation of my faults, that made me what I was. . . . (Stevenson 1979, p. 81)

We can see, from the wasting nature of Jekyll and his author, that it was not just hedonism that was so attractive, but the energy of life itself.

> My new power tempted me until I fell into slavery. I had but to drink the cup, and doff at once the body of the noted professor and to assume, like a thin cloak, that of Edward Hyde. (Ibid., p. 86)

There is a Calvinistic message in Stevenson's story, which I suspect became more moralistic with the revision. The message asserted is that Jekyll entertained hedonistic pursuits, thus giving strength to the beast within him. The beast was given license and made real through Jekyll's experiments with nature. Once he had cultivated the habit, the habit took over, dominating him and destroying him. This was a theme from the story that ministers often quoted from their pulpits in England and her colonies.

Hyde as Shadow

Mr. Hyde is the perfect representative of all that is repressed in a good man. He is "living in some city in a nightmare," with an "insensate readiness for evil." He is a constellation of a variety of vices, the most prominent of which is violent anger. Stevenson, like his character Jekyll, was always discreetly the gentleman, charming and notably considerate toward women and children. His violence found its voice in his adventure fiction and his "crawler" stories. Hyde, on the other hand, was not only violent, he pursued his pleasure "with bestial avidity." We see denial of this shadow in a statement in Jekyll's letter:

> Henry Jekyll stood at times aghast before the acts of Edward Hyde; but the situation was apart from ordinary laws, and insidiously relaxed the grasp of conscience. It was Hyde, after all, and Hyde alone, that was guilty. Jekyll was no worse; he woke again to his good qualities seemingly unimpaired; he would even make haste where it was possible, to undo the evil done by Hyde. (Stevenson 1979, p. 87)

And the primitiveness of the shadow, that unconscious being, is superbly described by Stevenson:

> He [Jekyll] thought of Hyde, for all the energy of life, as something not only hellish but inorganic. This was the shocking thing; that the slime of the pit seemed to utter cries and voices; and that what was dead, and had no shape, should usurp the offices of life. (Ibid., p. 95)

Yet, for all his depravity, it is Hyde's anger and his lack of compassion, his insensitivity to feelings for others, that lead to his identification in the first place and finally cause him to commit the crime of murder, which Jekyll at last cannot amend.

It seems contradictory that Hyde, given his "lust for life," should commit suicide. This may have been a choice that Stevenson, as author, made to conform to the Victorian mores that someone so evil should die. One could more easily envision Hyde being hunted down and killed than dying by his own hand. Fanny may have influenced Stevenson's choice of a final ending. Stevenson's father once advised the author to abide by Fanny's judgment in all that he published.

Energy Complexes

Jung, in his essay on the dynamics of the psyche, likened psychic energy to physical energy that arises as the result of the tension between opposite magnetic poles (1948a). Positive and negative electron exchanges in the passage of sodium and potassium in the neuron create the dynamo of opposites that generates the transmission of energy in the nervous system of the body. As described in chapter 1, the neurons in the brain connect at synapses to form maps as the result of experience, and these maps comprise the recognition system that we experience symbolically in dreams and imagination, and which we use to evaluate our experience of the outside world. When a neuronal map, which Jung referred to as a complex, recognizes an object, it responds and memory is activated. (See Edelman (1992) for a detailed Darwinist explanation of the brain.)

This connection between complex and object, then, may occur entirely within the psyche, or between the psyche and an object in the environment. The activation of a neuronal map resulting from such recognition is what Jung referred to as the constellation of a complex. For instance, when a person recognizes the familiar face of mother, the mother complex is constellated—the mother complex consisting of the memories of images and emotions associated to that person's experience of mother. Jung stated further that will was disposable energy—energy which we command from a conscious state. Symbols, on the other hand, can form without our willing them, coming from the energy of autonomous complexes, that is, complexes operating outside the ego's command. Traumas form complexes which are life-threatening (as seen by the ego), and this danger, I think, is what Hyde represented to Jekyll and to Robert Louis Stevenson.

Hyde was the complex of libido drive that threatened Robert Louis Stevenson, the author, and his character, Dr. Jekyll. Hyde was replete with moral ambiguity: the "slime of the pit" was also the life force. In this sense, Stevenson's nightmare resembles the trauma nightmare, which is both life-threatening and the source of intense energy which is blocked by repression from making a creative contribution. Indeed, the trauma nightmare may be a repetition of the state of hyper-arousal that reconstellates in the brain triggered by the generalized arousal of the normal REM stage of sleep associated most commonly with dreams (Ross et al. 1989). Terr thought of the repeating dream as pointing to psychic trauma (1990a, p. 209). It is the repetition of that trauma-generated state of hyper-arousal to which the psyche reacts, producing nightmare images; hence, the repetitive trauma nightmare and its variations. It is probably also this state of hyperarousal that makes the demarcation between consciousness and unconsciousness less certain. When what is going on in the brain is more stimulating than what is outside, one becomes occupied with the psychic image until it is superimposed like a map overlay onto the world, for example, the ghostly "presence" of the dead which can occur in the state of acute grief.

There seems to be no doubt that Stevenson was traumatized. He may have been traumatized more than once in his childhood because of medical procedures and prolonged recovery requiring critical care. Certainly his illness alone appears sufficient to have given him many life-threatening experiences.

It is in the nature of autonomous complexes, denied ego identification or even conscious awareness, that they are contaminated by unconscious contents. They hold what Jung, in *Psychology and Alchemy* (1944), referred to as the intensely fertile *prima materia*. We note the unanimous reaction of others to Hyde, that he is in some undefinable way deformed. Enfield described him:

> There is something wrong with his appearance; something displeasing, something downright detestable. I never saw a man I so disliked, and yet I scarce know why. He must be deformed somewhere; he gives a strong feeling of deformity, although I couldn't specify the point. (Stevenson 1979, p. 34)

The trauma complex has all the power of the trauma experience. That power is cumulative as the traumas repeat. One can see the intensity of the trauma complex displayed in the overreactive affect of a threatened adult who was repeatedly abused as a child. Robert Louis Stevenson was repeatedly abused by nature through his respiratory illness. He was a lively man whose energy would kill him if he was not careful. Hyde symbolized his trauma complex.

Trauma as Archetype

Culture is a collection of psyches interacting and creating one large collective consciousness, which has the same characteristics as its parts, and then some. The collective psyche would be less intelligent than about half its members, given that collectively the individual IQs would regress toward the mean, but would be more powerful than any single member. The period in which Robert Louis Stevenson lived was significant for its transition to modern urban industrialism. England's industrial global dominance was at its peak when Stevenson wrote "The Strange Case of Dr. Jekyll and Mr. Hyde." The Victorian period was remarkable for the rise of the middle class. Issues like incest, child abuse, and spousal battering were not discussed in private, much less in public. In a society bound by convention and full of strictures both private and public, Stevenson struck a collective chord in the public's enthusiasm for the story, which no doubt for many released the shadow to their view. The publication of the book was, in some respects, a cultural "primal experience," of the sort that Homer would have taken to mean the appearance of a deity (Otto 1954). In 1886, when the book was first published, it sold forty thousand copies in six weeks in England alone. It was also an immediate hit in the United States, where it was sold in pirated editions and was preached from the pulpit. The story eventually took on a life of its own, divorced from its author. It may be a hallmark of archetypal literature that it becomes identified by itself and not as having been written by anyone in particular.

One of Stevenson's social companions at the time of writing "Dr. Jekyll and Mr. Hyde" was the son of Mary Shelley, author of *Frankenstein*. One of several remarkable documents about arrogance as the shadow of science, *Frankenstein* is a story of the doctor's error of raising the dead, which was the act of arrogance (or inflated compassion) that cost Aesculapius his life. Stevenson himself had several collisions with science, and medicine was the branch of science most directly touching him, having brutalized him with superstition. Thus, the theme of medicine is apparent throughout the story. Hyde is introduced trampling a child who is running for a doctor. Hyde appeared to Jekyll's colleague Lanyon and claimed professional confidentiality before revealing his other identity. Jekyll conducted his experiments in cabinets behind an anatomical surgery theater where a famous surgeon had demonstrated his technique before students. Hyde eventually became a conscious identity through a chemical accident and not through the process of logical deduction. Dr. Lanyon refers to Jekyll's research as heretical and calls Jekyll "flighty," a term that must also have been applied to Stevenson. Ironically, Jekyll refers to Lanyon as a "hidebound pedant." Hyde taunts Lanyon with his "transcendental medicine," in a remarkable speech that, on the threshold of the atomic age, succinctly sets forth the implications of choosing the path of science. Hyde says:

> Will you be wise? Will you be guided? Will you suffer me to take this glass in my hand and go forth from your house without further parley? Or has the greed of curiosity too much command of you? Think before you answer, for it shall be done as you decide. As you decide, you shall be left as you were before, and neither richer nor wiser, unless the sense of service rendered to a man in mortal distress may be counted as a kind of riches of the soul. Or, if you shall so prefer to choose, a new province of knowledge and new avenues of fame and power shall be laid open to you here, in this room, upon the instant; and your sight shall be blasted by a prodigy to stagger the unbelief of Satan. (Stevenson 1979, p. 79)

Stevenson spent his last years traveling with his extended family in the South Pacific, where Father Damien dedicated his life to working with lepers and died of the disease himself. Stevenson admired Father Damien, and when a preacher in Australia made the press with a denunciation of Damien as a coarse, dirty, headstrong, bigoted man who contracted leprosy by having sex with lepers, Stevenson wrote a letter in defense of the priest. Stevenson so thoroughly attacked this preacher, whose name was Hyde, that he feared prosecution for libel.

Stevenson collaborated with W. E. Henley in writing a play, which turned out poorly, about an Edinburgh character named Deacon Brodie. Brodie was a respected cabinetmaker by day and a leader of a gang of robbers by night. Stevenson was alleged to have grown up with a Deacon Brodie cabinet in his room. He was collaborating on the play at the time he wrote "The Strange Case of Dr. Jekyll and Mr. Hyde." Fanny thought Henley was draining Stevenson. Hyde, recall, committed suicide in Jekyll's cabinets.

The dark side of medicine, of course, is traumatic abuse, which can be seen by examining the negative side of the Aesculapius story outlined in chapter 2. As the demigod of medicine, we think of him as a healer with knowledge of earth's mysteries. We prefer not to think of Aesculapius as being born of trauma, being taken from his mother's womb on her funeral pyre by his father, her murderer; and we prefer not to think of Aesculapius as going too far with his healing arts, raising the dead and the ire of Zeus.

Robert Louis Stevenson experienced the traumatic side of medicine. Scientific medicine facilitated the abuse of nature on his being and probably gave him an opium addiction to accompany his near-death experiences. He was literally and figuratively trampled by his illness and his treatments. His psychic energy greatly exceeded his physical strength (as perhaps it had all his life). Propriety did not let him talk about his sexuality. It did let him portray violent anger, "bestial avidity," and lusting appetite in his fiction.

Persons who experience trauma, whether as children or adults, whatever the circumstances, have a sense of the power of the emergency activating system that creates full physiological arousal, clarifies vision, and gives one a narrow focus of attention. The trauma survivor has immediate knowledge of a terrible epiphany, a peak experience that has blasted away old boundaries of knowledge, leaving the survivor with a memory of pain and terror. As Terr observes, "the idea of trauma is to feel plain, very normal, and then to be mowed down with something extraordinary" (1990a, p. 382).

Stevenson lived in a culture that had trampled Ireland and was causing the Irish to starve. It was similarly subjecting and exploiting other overseas colonies at the height of its imperial power. Hyde can be seen as a metaphor for habit, individual or collective denial, and a simultaneous covert exercise of shadow. Hyde's last speech ("Will you be wise? Will you be guided?") evokes the fear of science without moral restraint, which is certainly a metaphor for the power of the shadow as representative of the individual unconscious. The real collective problem is that the threat of nuclear destruction (science unchecked) is alive today—and denied pathologically (Wear 1987). What proves to be the problem of the individual trauma survivor—integration of the trauma—is the problem of Western culture in our age, namely integration of the collective shadow. It is depicted in Stevenson's story and nightmare as his problem, the problem of having the knowledge of energy that can destroy its beholder.

Summary

Robert Louis Stevenson's unwanted consciousness is represented in Edward Hyde. His trauma complex was contaminated with unconscious, repressed, life-threatening energy, partly sexual, partly violent anger, that eventually destroyed itself. Hyde was personified to Stevenson in a nightmare and turned into a literary masterpiece that continues to catch the eye of modern Western culture. Stevenson saw Victorian imperial England at its worst and, as he showed with his stories and his life, identified with the trampled child. Stevenson so captured a collective archetype that his story has virtually become a folk tale.

Trauma to children has been amply described in fairy tales through the centuries, and these tales have become the lesson plans for trauma recovery. The most common of psychogical traumas, the premature or precipitous loss of a parent and traumas committed by a parent, will be discussed in the next three chapters.

Chapter 6

"The fairy tale . . . represents extremely well the working of our psyche: what our psychological problems are, and how these can best be mastered. . . . For example, many fairy stories begin with the death of a mother or father; in these tales the death of the parent creates the most agonizing problems . . . ."
Bettelheim, *The Uses of Enchantment*

CINDERELLA, SNOW WHITE, AND TRAUMA FROM THE MOTHER

There are several hundred versions of Snow White and Cinderella found around thc world. They are archetypal expressions of a human situation, the plight of a girl who loses her mother. Although the situations they describe cannot be limited to one interpretation, ubiquitous folk tales such as these describe well a very human situation.

When a girl loses her mother, a crisis of ego development occurs that is usually traumatic, especially if a girl is abandoned by her mother suddenly, under circumstances that were unexpected, and trauma would occur even if the girl didn't like her mother. In fact, emotional conflict with the mother may complicate and prolong grief and recovery. Generally, however, the better the mother, the greater the loss.

Girls depend on their mothers to help them determine

their identities. Their fathers' principle role is a more unconscious influence. It is far more devastating for a girl to be abused by her mother than her father. This is not intended to minimize abuse by the father, but only to say that the two types of parental trauma have different symptomatic expressions. (The next chapter addresses trauma from the father.) Generally speaking, abuse by the parent who is the same sex as the child has a direct impact on the identity of the child in the same traumatic way that abandonment or sudden loss would have. While abuse by the opposite-sexed parent creates an enemy, abuse by the same-sexed parent causes the enemy to be lodged within the ego itself. When a girl becomes traumatized by her mother, even if the trauma is passive, as when a mother is never emotionally available for her daughter, the girl's sense of secure identity is severely shaken, and the trauma disorder becomes an ongoing source of existential anxiety. The loss of mother becomes a serious setback in development, significant at any age, and particularly significant during adolescence. The trauma partially arrests development, and the trauma complex retains a piece of the personality of that age. Bowlby describes the traumatic effects of the loss of mother in adolescent girls (Bowlby 1988).

While the loss of mother directly affects a girl's identity, the loss of father creates unconscious drives that affect the way she thinks about relationships, society, and the future. (When the trauma is devastating, her identity is crushed in any case.) The loss of father and abuse by the father affect school, marriage, career ambitions and planning, and the way one relates to institutions. If the child is protected by the nonabusive parent, the trauma disorder is mitigated somewhat.

The crucial determinant in parental trauma (when the parent, knowingly or not, directly traumatizes the child) is the age and cognitive development of the child. Age has to do with what (if any) images contribute to the trauma complex, which in turn plays a part in how the trauma emotions are interpreted. The earlier the trauma in a child's life, the less specific is the trauma imagery and the more the symptoms seem part of the child's personality. Mary Shelley is an example mentioned in previous chapters of one who lost her mother at an early age, a trauma that unconsciously shaped her literary career (Mellor 1988). The trauma complex, as described in chapter 1, consists of the emotions and images elicited by the repeating of the hyperarousal state that occurs at the time of the trauma. This developmental difference can be seen in the mother traumas of Cinderella and Snow White, as depicted in the Grimms' fairy tales.

Cinderella

When Cinderella is traumatized by her mother's death (it is unclear at what age), she is impoverished and meanly treated by her stepfamily. The abuse is entirely feminine, coming from stepmother and stepsisters. Cinderella's "rich" father is a virtual nonentity in the story. If he bore Cinderella ill will, it was by unconsciously abusing her by marrying an abusive woman.

Cinderella keeps alive her mother's spirit, which is transmitted through her mother's own words. Before dying, her mother spoke to her, invoking God's protection and adding significantly, "and I will look down on you from heaven and be near you." Her mother complex (memories and emotions associated with her mother) will thus influence and guide her as a source of wisdom and comfort. Jung writes of spirit complexes:

> So far as I can judge, these experiences [intruding spirits] occur either when something so devastating happens to the individual that his whole previous attitude to life breaks down, or when for some reason the contents of the collective unconscious accumulate so much energy that they start influencing the conscious mind. (Jung 1948a, par. 594)

One might call "Cinderella" the story of a Hestia complex because she is bound to the hearth and turns to the spirit for comfort (Demetrapoulas 1979). Her trials are all domestic. She is charged with the maintenance of the fire, the fetching of water, and the cooking and washing for the family. Her name is a nickname, Cinder-ella (*Ashenputtel*) because she sleeps by the hearth, and her stepsisters abuse her by throwing lentils into the ashes. Ashes, as Bettelheim notes, suggest mourning (1989a, p. 255).

There are more than seven hundred versions of Cinderella worldwide. Perrault's seventeenth-century version is the most popular and the one adopted by Disney Studios. His Cinderella was written at the behest of and for consumption by the French literate aristocracy (Tatar 1987). In this version, the fairy godmother is created as a symbol of the mother spirit. The negative mother complex in most versions is typically depicted in triune form—reminiscent of the moon goddess, Hecate (later differentiated as Artemis, Demeter, and Kore)—by the stepmother and her two daughters. The negative form is thus one "step" removed from her identity. Other versions give Cinderella an "unnatural," i.e., wicked father (ibid., p. 153).

The process by which Cinderella in the Grimms' version contacts her mother's spirit is interesting. Her rich father is going to a fair and asks his daughters what they want him to bring back. Cinderella asks for "the first branch that knocks against your hat on the way home." He brings her back a hazel branch. Hazel is remarkable in European folklore as a source of spiritual knowledge. It was prized as a divining tool and was sewn into clothing to speed recovery. It was considered sacred to Hermes-Mercury, the soul guide. Cinderella takes the branch and plants it on her mother's grave. She waters it with her tears, the branch grows into a "handsome" tree, and a bird alights in the tree. The bird "threw down to her what she had wished for" (Grimm and Grimm 1972).

Thus, through the girl's grief for her mother comes the spiritual inspiration. Her father is the vehicle for contacting her mother. He helps her, not directly by giving her a gift, but significantly by giving her what she wishes for. The crucial gift from the father is not to tell his daughter what to do, because he doesn't really know what's good for her, but to give her freedom and support.

Cinderella's state of poverty and abuse is certainly a symbol of depression. The abuse coming from the feminine can be seen symbolically as compulsive thoughts that demean female self-image, physically manifesting as an obsession with physical beauty, shape, or form, in eating disorders, in compulsive perfectionism, and in self-mutilation and suicidal impulses. Trauma from and to the female does not require the obvious abuse by or death of the mother. Loss of mother may come quite symbolically through the mother's own neurotic emotional withdrawal from her daughter. While such loss may not qualify as PTSD in the diagnostic manual, it can manifest with the intensity of a trauma complex as a significant emotional experience. The mother may herself have been traumatized and arrested in her own development, alcoholic, emotionally and intellectually absent, physically ill, or merely too often missing.

Loss of mother in childhood for children of either sex is a loss of what mother gives; it is a trauma of nurturance. While the loss of mother for the female child is crucial to ego development and physical identity, the loss of mother for the male is one of spiritual or unconscious anima, creating in the male a quest for the female nurturer in sexual obsession or creative pursuit. Such a male may be as obsessed with the female body as the traumatized female, but his obsession is usually interpreted sexually.

Cinderella's depression is different from the naive wandering that we see in Snow White. She is the abused stepchild until she is able to access her mother's spirit (godmother) and establish her own identity. When she can do this, she enhances her image and becomes beautiful.

Snow White

Snow White loses her mother at birth. This is significiant because she has no way to contact her mother in her memory. Her wicked stepmother is not the crudely abusive hag of domestic violence, but the wicked, vain queen who stands in competition with Snow White, as Morgan of the Arthurian romance stood in competition with Guinevere. Snow White's stepmother is known throughout the story as "the Queen." Tatar states that in Grimms' initial edition the wicked queen was Snow White's natural mother (1987, p. 143). She gives Snow White to a hunter to be taken into the forest and killed, because the girl is said by the looking glass to be the most beautiful in the land. The existence of the vain Queen threatens the existence of Snow White, just as in a dream enemies vie with the ego. Snow White is named after just one of her three primary colors, the others being blood red and raven black, the passion and death, respectively, which form her opposition. (Little Red Riding Hood, Cinderella, and Snow White would form a complete triad.) Graves, in discussing the title of his book, *The White Goddess,* notes:

> I write of her as the White Goddess because white is her principle colour, the colour of the first member of her moon-trinity . . . the New Moon is the white goddess of birth and growth; the Full Moon, the red goddess of love and battle; the Old Moon, the black goddess of death and divination. Graves 1948, p. 70)

Elsewhere, Graves writes again of the triune goddess and quotes a folk poem:

> As the New Moon or Spring she was the girl; as the Full Moon or Summer she was woman; as the Old Moon or Winter she was hag.
>
> "Diana in the leaves green,
> Luna that so bright doth sheen,
> Persephone in Hell." (Ibid., p. 386)

Snow White, losing her mother at birth, has a mother complex that does not include the imagery of a unified good mother to guide her. The Queen orders a hunter to take the girl into the forest and kill her, and, in what is a female variant of "Sir Gawain and the Green Knight," she is instead let loose by the hunter and wanders in the wilderness (her depression) until she comes upon the home of the seven dwarfs. No one is home, but their tables are laid for eating. Snow White eats, for she is hungry, but takes only a little from each, with moderation, and avails herself of their cozy sleeping accommodations.

Snow White is helped, as it were, by an unconscious that is represented as fragmented, dwarfish, and masculine. Her mother trauma is so profoundly basic and imageless because it occurred at birth. The traumas of birth, such as birth crisis, incubator confinement, strangulation, and mutilation, as noted in chapter 1, leave no intellectual component but cause a profound midbrain experience, a primary stimulation that becomes a body memory. This traumatic stimulation repeats in the life of the survivor as a trauma disorder that may go undiagnosed, but leaves in the adult "a life-long dread to be avoided and feared" (Krystal 1988, p. 147). For Snow White to lose her mother when she most needed her creates a life-threatening theme.

Snow White, in exile with the dwarfs, is charged with domestic chores, caring for the seven dwarfs, but this work she does "with all my heart," because they are friendly and "asked what her name was," thus respecting her identity. Snow White here might be seen as the oldest girl in a family whose mother is absent, a family nonetheless well enough adjusted to continue to function cohesively; she adopts the mother role in a pretend way (caring for little men). Or she might be seen as the girl from a pathogenic family who avoids home and takes up with outlaws, becomes a rock groupie or team follower. Mary Shelley was living in exile and vacationing with her three dwarfs (Percy Shelly, Lord Byron, and Dr. Polidori) when she wrote her novel about the "hideous progeny" born without a mother (Mellor 1988). In all such cases of early mother loss, the identity of the survivor is dependent on multiple others.

The only mother Snow White knows is the negative Queen who is archetypal and lethal. Snow White must compete with the wicked Queen and not even know she is doing it. While Cinderella's abuse comes through impossible chores, Snow White's comes by threat to her very existence. She is attacked with secret poison, which weakens her toward death, each time she compulsively opens the door. In the sense that Snow White has been traumatized, she is helpless in dealing with a trauma disorder that operates unconsciously. Bolen (1984, p. 211) refers to Snow White as a Persephone girl, but it is deceptive to think of Snow White as comprising a Persephone personality; Persephone is but one of the dynamic characters in Snow White's psyche. Bolen refers to Cinderella also as a passive Persephone girl, but Cinderella is hardly passive, although she certainly does her time in "Hell," patiently sorting through the ashes. She has a mother spirit that is helpful and with whom she communicates, as Demeter communicates with Persephone through Hermes.

The Process of Sorting

The process of sorting is akin to Gawain's quest for the Green Knight's chapel in which he endures the challenges of hardship and threats of death. While "Snow White" and "Cinderella" concern the feminine, they are not exclusively women's. Tatar notes that until modern times, there were virtually interchangable male and female versions of these tales (1987, p. 47). These stories do concern feminine development, however. Just as the woman (albeit identified with and dedicated to the goddess) must deal with the hero myths when she crosses into the masculine realm and opts for a competitive career (as did Camilla in the *Aeneid*), the man must deal with the female goddesses when he crosses, voluntarily or not, into the feminine. Trauma for the male opens a channel to his own unconscious that is represented as feminine and sometimes feels distorted (dwarflike) when it first comes to consciousness. One traumatized veteran, on being urged to send flowers to his wife, finally did so and announced to his group that he felt "like a dork." A gay man may be a Cinderella to his wicked stepsisters, his gay lovers, and be forever sorting lentils from the ashes, trying to access his spiritual mother through his troublesome mother complex. A mother-dominated, father-abandoned straight man may undertake an unconscious quest for perfection, which amounts to obsessional sorting.

Cinderella and Snow White are each saved by a prince, but in quite different ways. Cinderella, whose mother trauma occurred as a child, actively seeks her mother through her trauma complex as a source of inspiration, accessed and made available through grief. She acquires a beautiful dress from her mother spirit, which represents the enhancement of the female image. Her grief is a process of working through and consciously assimilating the trauma. She then proceeds to attend the ball and attract the prince, who is the reborn king—the divine masculine symbol for the so-called royal *coniunctio*, thus activating the woman's creative unconscious.

Snow White, whose mother trauma occurred at birth, must go about the recovery process passively and unconsciously. Note that Snow White is repeatedly opening her door to the Queen disguised as an old woman, remaining maddeningly naive to her guises. She is nearly murdered by the Queen when she is put into a deathlike trance and placed in a glass coffin by the dwarfs, who cannot bear to place her in the darkness when her beauty does not diminish with death. Because she had no guiding mother spirit, the Queen had easy access to influence her ego identity. (This topic will be more completely discussed in chapter 8.)

The dwarfs place Snow White on a mountain where birds come to weep (notably an owl, a raven, and lastly a dove, signifying a progression toward integration). She is brought back to life by accident. When the prince claims her, the dwarfs, bringing her glass coffin down the mountain, drop her. The Queen's poison apple bite is dislodged from her throat, and she is revived. Chance, the trickster of nature, rules her fate.

In contrast to Snow White's passivity, Cinderella can make an ego decision to enhance her identity with the aid of her mother's spiritual dove, to overcome the troublesome obsessions, and seek and marry the king's son. This represents the working through of trauma and finding the value in the mother complex. For the girl who loses or is abused by mother, this process is terribly difficult and even deadly. Jung describes the divine marriage as a spiritual relationship between the conscious and the unconscious, here between the woman's conscious identity in creative relationship with her unconscious.

Snow White has no personalized mother complex, which makes contacting her mother complex a spiritual dilemma, because it is entirely trauma-associated and unconscious. Snow White's relationship to it is toxic and dangerous. The Queen, a complex of self-destruction, attacks her with enchanted laces which squeeze her breathless, a poisonous comb that places her in a trance, and an apple that she chokes on, each more deadly than the last. When the Queen wanted the hunter to kill Snow White, she asked for the girl's lungs and liver to be returned as evidence. The hunter killed a boar instead and gave the girl to wild nature. The lungs and liver symbolize the mechanisms of transformation and growth: spirit from the lungs and nurturance from the liver, especially the ability to separate poison from food. With the first two attacks, the Queen, disguised as a peddler woman, tells Snow White her appearance is wrong and pretends to correct the problem, bringing Snow White close to death. On the third visit, she gives Snow White a classic eating disorder with the apple that is as pretty as she is (white and red). The compulsivity of an eating disorder reflects an ego that is weaker than the negative mother complex. Snow White never feels certain about her self-image because she has no real mother as a model. She is nurtured and protected by her unconscious denial, which saves her from devastation, but the denial also fragments her personality and stops her emotional growth.

The Dwarfs

In "Snow White," the dwarfs represent the feminine unconscious in undifferentiated form. The dwarfs are little miners. Disney gave the dwarfs comic identities and had them whistle while they worked, which is a kind of Americanization of the fieldworker dwarfs of European folklore. In the Snow White story, the dwarfs are all male, although in European folklore there are female dwarfs. Girls who remain stuck at Snow White's level give themselves over to the unconscious, which is, of course, projected onto society and culture. Hephaestus, the Greek god of mining and metallurgy, had a gnomelike countenance. He was considered ugly and was said to be lame as the result of his mother's (Hera's) abrupt abandonment. He could be said to be the god of mother trauma, and as such, the guide and healer of those so traumatized. Hephaestus is doubly applicable here, because he was conceived and born of his mother alone.

The modern Western drug culture provides ample characters to populate the equivalent of a dwarf culture for the children of trauma. As denizens of an underworld or counter-culture, they give the illusion of being perpetually young. Besides having eating or drug abuse (toxic poisoning) disorders, the children of trauma may find themselves obsessed with gangs, sports teams, or rock groups, to which they devote themselves to the sacrifice of their own identities. Such obsessional devotion is not the same thing as interest and is not exclusively female, by any means, but represents a projection of the fragmented unconscious.

Disney's euphemistic revisionism obscures a dark, phallic aspect of dwarfs in Greek and Roman myths. Living with the dwarfs, Snow White enters a chthonic environment that suggests a state of enchantment, or suspension of growth, that is a refuge from the Queen while she awaits an awakening of consciousness in order to develop further.

Examples of Mother Trauma

I will present here briefly three cases. One is a treatment case that is basically fictional, although based on many cases or combinations of people I have known who have been traumatized by loss of mother. The second is a case from contemporary culture, and the third example is drawn from another fairy tale.

Iris

Iris had a mean-spirited mother who chose to "work and have fun" rather than go to college. When her mother married and had children, she did not enjoy motherhood. Iris said that her mother favored her firstborn son, who became a successful professional, while emotionally snubbing her daughter. When Iris was eleven, her mother left her with her father and uncle and went off on a month's vacation with a girlfriend. Iris thinks that she was sexually molested by her uncle at that time but can recall only very vague details. After that, however, Iris developed a tightness in her tongue that inhibited her speech and an acne skin condition that caused her much distress. She said that her mother was not willing to talk about sex or female development. She could just as easily have developed some other somatic or behavioral symptom to express the emotion of her mother's abandonment.

In response to her mother's dominating behavior, Iris

developed an obsessive-compulsive style that demanded perfection in her chores, a practice which was particularly maddening for her impatient mother. Iris was socially introverted and remained fairly isolated through college. It seemed as though she was able to develop self-esteem around intellectual and logical thought processes but developed only very limited emotional flexibility and depth. She found sex very difficult, and she chose to marry a man who was in many ways her opposite. When we discussed fairy tales, she thought of her husband as her helpful animal, who loved her only because she put order in his life.

Iris quickly saw the relevance of her mother's meanness and emotional abandonment. She referred to her mother as "being unavailable." She had experienced her anger at her mother and her uncle (her father was a passive man who remained in the background and died during her adolescence) as angry dreams and fantasy images of mutilation and mayhem, which largely dissipated as she began to discuss her feelings. She felt nurtured by having her emotions attended to, but getting her to nurture herself was a more difficult matter.

Iris appears to have been traumatized both by the abandonment of her mother and by sexual abuse from her uncle. The classical fairy-tale motif is played out profoundly when a girl loses touch with her mother at the time she is traumatized. When a girl is traumatized, she needs her mother at an extra level of emotional profundity, and if she cannot contact her mother at that depth, as Iris could not, she has to deal with the trauma complex on her own at the expense of her feminine development.

Iris's father did not help her, but her husband seemed to bring her what she needed most, emotional warmth and playfulness, which created a delicate and precarious balance for her stern, saturnine disposition. When her therapist gave her the safety of a therapeutic structure, she could begin to integrate the trauma of her mother's abandonment. Her feelings about her mother were hard for her to sort out and integrate, but the process was necessary preceding the work on the frightful ambiguity of her uncle's suspected advances.

Art

The late jazz saxophonist Art Pepper gives us a male version of "Snow White" in his autobiographical account, *Straight Life* (Pepper and Pepper 1979). He was an unwanted child; his mother tried to abort him ("I was born. She lost"). He recounts scenes of early abandonment by both parents and the witnessing of violent fights between them. "My parents always fought. He broke her nose several times" (ibid., p. 5). He was put in his grandmother's care but "saw there was no warmth, no affection. I was terrified and completely alone. At that time I realized that no one wanted me. There was no love and I wished I could die" (ibid.). He reports being treated with medication for nightmares in childhood. His career is remarkable for his brilliant jazz improvisation, his sexual appetite, his opiate addiction, and related thievery and legal punishments. He spent many years in California prisons.

With Art, as in many examples of mother trauma, traumas from the father or others increase the need for the nurturing mother. In Art's case, the father was clearly abusive. He once beat him with a belt when, after being forced to eat, the boy gagged and vomited. This was the same father who bought him his first saxophone and encouraged his interest. But what was crucial to his opiate addiction and early death was the traumatic combination of his mother's abandonment and his father's abuse. Art was cast out into the wilderness, so to speak. He was taken up and cared for by the jazz and drug underground of the 1940s and 1950s, members of which played the role of the dwarfs in his story.

Elsa

A case of coping with abuse from the mother is found in "The Tale of the Tontlawald," which is in Lang's collection of fairy stories (1966). In this story, Elsa's mother died and her step-mother "beat and cuffed the poor child from morning till night" (p. 2). Elsa was warned away from an enchanted wood, the Tontlawald, but entered it anyway, because the dwellers could be no worse than her stepmother. There she met a fairy child who took Elsa to "the Lady of the Tontlawald." Elsa asked to stay because her stepmother would "half kill" her for being away. The fairies adopted Elsa. The fairy queen had "a little old man" make a replica of Elsa to send back to her stepmother "that she may beat it instead of you. Let her flog it as hard as she will, it can never feel any pain . . ." (p. 9). The little old man put a snake and a piece of bread into the doll of Elsa. The snake eventually killed the stepmother, when the wicked woman tried to strangle Elsa's replica. Elsa's father, who did nothing to protect the girl, ate the piece of bread and died, too.

The problem with Elsa's situation was that the fairies with whom she sought refuge did not grow as she did. Eventually she had to leave the Tontlawald (she flew out, transformed into a bird) and when she "recovered her senses," she met a handsome prince, who had been searching for her because he had dreamed that he would find her. Elsa eventually became queen, "and when she was old she told this story" (Lang 1966, p. 16).

This tale is an example of the traumatized child who flees into fantasy to escape the pain of the abuse, leaving behind a numb replica of herself to be beaten. It is also an example of the dissociative aspect of trauma disorder, in which the split-off personalities, functioning as refuges from abuse, do not grow with the ego complex. The child must eventually leave them behind and return to the human world to achieve wholeness. When she does this, her animus prince can find her, and she can develop creatively.

Summary

Mother trauma may be passive or active and may come from abuse directly applied to the child or from abandonment in body or spirit, and does not depend on the character of the mother. Mother trauma can occur simply from the death of the parent. Mother trauma to a girl is an ego identity wound and the negative impact directly threatens the female image. If the trauma occurs early in infancy, the trauma complex is without intellectual imagery. Mother trauma later in childhood at least allows the child to process some positive aspect of the mother complex to reach wholeness. The fairy tales of "Cinderella" and "Snow White" show us the different problems created by mother trauma, as they apply to the surviving child dealing with a hostile world. Mother trauma becomes a problem of nurturance and care for one's self. Mother trauma to a boy is more a social, sexual, and unconscious problem. Mother trauma to a girl threatens the very existence of her identity.

In the next chapter the problem of father trauma is considered, specifically the gender difference of the impact of father trauma and trauma as superconditioning.

Chapter 7

THE MALE MONSTER AND TRAUMA FROM THE FATHER

When the father is traumatically abusive, the male child incorporates the abusive image and tends to identify himself as the perpetrator of violence. His model for manhood is also the man who trains his responses to problem-solving with violent conditioning. *Super conditioning* is a term used by Pitman (1989) to describe the hyperarousal of trauma that becomes associated with random variables, i.e., objects, images, and experiences connected to the trauma and subsumed into the trauma complex. When trauma becomes associated with an already existing powerful complex, the complex itself takes on the quality of a drive. Trauma gives the complex a motivating force that directs behavior. When the complex is stimulated by an archetype, it has the power of fate. Warriors like Gawain fight because of a father complex and the father complex then becomes a supercharged father/trauma complex.

When the father complex becomes a trauma complex, father becomes the male beast. The father-traumatized male identifies with the father and becomes like the beast. The father-traumatized female experiences the father complex as an unconscious animus drive that is bestial.

Women with Trauma from the Father

Unlike the male child, a girl rarely identifies herself as a violent person when she is abused by father. Her identification with the aggressor takes place unconsciously, causing her to project the abuser onto an abusive society.

One example of a woman with a bestial trauma-driven animus was Beatrice, a very successful professional woman, who repeatedly dreamed of a male monster coming to get her. His form changed from dream to dream. Occasionally, he would appear as a known figure. Usually he was vaguely seen as out there or vividly etched as a psychopathic criminal. This woman had had an overbearing father whose discipline was brutal mainly because of his size and his rigidity. What she described from her nightmares, however, was not father, but the father as trauma complex that drove her to achieve. Her life's goal was to strive for perfection and never to be weak. She worked for a rigidly hierarchical, male-dominated institution, where no women had ever been promoted to high positions of authority. Her written work was flawless but she tended to be chronically behind because she spent so much time on each report. I thought of her as a female warrior in a man's army and told her the story of the Latin warrior, Camilla.

Camilla, who was abandoned by her mad father, King Metabus, in Virgil's *Aeneid*, was caught up in a competitive male-dominated world. Camilla was renowned as a runner so swift that she would dash across the top of a wheat field without bending the grain. (Beatrice ran three miles every morning around a lake before work.) Dedicated to Minerva, Camilla was killed while fighting the exiled Trojans, shot from a crowd by Arruns, the archetypal coward. Minerva sent Iris to seek revenge on Arruns.

A historical example of a father-dominated woman is Mary Shelley (née Godwin). Discussed earlier as a girl who lost her mother early, she was dominated by her rebellious father (considered by many of his contemporaries to be as mad as King Metabuse) until she ran away with the bohemian Percy Shelley. Although she competed with men, Mellor (1989) shows that she submitted to her husband's authority as editor and literary advisor. Her beast, Frankenstein's monster, her "hideous progeny," is a male, born by a male without women and rejected by the world and by his own father. Mary Shelley's father rejected her when she ran off with Percy and his entourage. Within her psyche was the monster that she projected as a spontaneous phantasm.

The paradox implied in these examples is that the woman who was dominated as a child by an abusive father is driven to compete in a male-dominated world where she must submit to the rule of the males in charge. Beatrice described her mother as kind and perpetually giving, and deferring in a traditional way to her husband's authority. Camilla's mother died when she was young. Mary Shelley's famous mother also died when she was born. None of these women was able to identify their power as coming from the feminine. It was only through psychotherapy that Beatrice could emotionally accept the feminine as powerful.

In 1991 a film was released that captured the imagination of Beatrice as well as many other American women. *Thelma and Louise* depicts two women who have been traumatized by men. Louise kills the man attempting to rape Thelma and in slaying him seems to be responding to a rage impulse from her own trauma past. In truly American fashion, the rapist tells Louise to "suck his cock," and she shoots him dead. The manslaughter launches them into a desperado world, for which Thelma at least seems to develop a taste. In the course of their escape, they are hounded on the highway by an animal-man driving a polished steel truck, remarkably without a corporate logo but with stainless steel images of bimbos on his mud flaps. The women are finally (and literally) driven over the edge by a battle line of males with guns. In the final chase scene, it seems that the Hollywood male beast has succeeded in dominating the film with tasteless, but commercial, sensationalism.

Beatrice was on the verge of competing to her death. As she entered middle age, she lived alone in a barren apartment, worked very long hours, receiving work-related phone calls at night, and feared that work would kill her. She couldn't stand the idea of taking an extended vacation and having her co-workers think of her as a softy. The effects of her father's abuse had instilled in her a drive that was archetypal.

Beauty and the Beast and the Prince Behind Him

When paleontologists use the term *archetype,* they refer to the concept of the one in the many, in evolutionary terms, the basic mold from which many forms evolved (Gould 1991). When Jung refers to the archetype, he refers to the single psychological image, experience, or action that has fit the collective human condition down through the eons. Archetype is a product of the evolving human brain and is genetically inherited. Jung (1949) contends that the physical genesis of the father archetype, for instance, is anticipated by the inherited shape of the brain. Jung described the father archetype as releasing a "fateful power" when a man becomes so dominant that he identifies with the archetype. He writes:

> The danger is just this unconscious identity with the archetype: not only does it exert a dominating influence on the child, so that it succumbs to the influence from outside and at the same time cannot oppose it from within. (Jung 1949, par. 729)

Thus, the more the father is possessed by the father archetype, the more powerful his influence on the children, and the more his sons and daughters are dominated and compelled.

The male beast is the "father animal," a mythological motif in which the father appears as threatening and is projected onto the world as the male beast. Culture, when it is dominated by the father archetype, becomes the male monster.

Jung thought of fairy tales and mythology as expressive of archetypal situations, i.e., the archetypal image in action. These tales are repeatedly told because they are expressive of common human plight across cultures and spanning generations. The story of coming to terms with the male beast as an example of this archetypal situation can be found in the French literary fairy tales, told and retold by peasants, recorded in writing for the literary elite, and then used as lessons for the general public (Zipes 1989). A tale that uses the father/monster motif is "Beauty and the Beast."

Like all the best fairy tales, "Beauty and the Beast" operates on two levels. One level addresses real-life situations of people, specifically girls leaving home at their fathers' direction, while the other level is a description of individual psychological process. "Beauty and the Beast," a commonly told tale in the eighteenth century, was recorded in two very different styles, by two very different women. The tale was about a common dilemma for women of their time, and each version reflects the author's individual experiences as well. The real-life situations, depicted from the perspective of eighteenth-century women, is the dilemma faced by young women who married men most likely not of their choosing but at the behest of their fathers and who were dependent on their fathers and husbands for their security. The story of "Beauty and the Beast" was written by one author, Jeanne-Marie Leprince de Beaumont, as a lesson for the proper upbringing of girls (Zipes 1989, p. 233).

The first version, "The Story of Beauty and the Beast," was written by Gabrielle-Suzanne de Villeneuve and first published in 1740 (Zipes 1989, p. 153). A second, shorter version, was written a short time later by Leprince de Beaumont and published in 1757 in a collection of lessons for girls, a kind of chapbook. Both women had been married briefly to older men. De Villeneuve married an army colonel who died soon thereafter. Leprince de Beaumont married a "dissolute libertine" at the age of thirty-two and her marriage was annulled two years later.

The two versions of "Beauty and the Beast" are quite different in style. The de Villeneuve version is elaborate, ornate, courtly, lengthy, and baroque. Leprince de Beaumont's story is brief, far more economical and artistically pleasing. Both versions of the tale present the beast as stupid and ugly, capable of ferocity, but not mean or cruel ("more stupid than ferocious"). As Beauty observes in Leprince de Beaumont's version: "There are many men who are more monstrous than you" (Zipes 1989, p. 240). In both versions, the beast threatens suicide by entering his grief-stricken decline if Beauty leaves him. In both versions, the beast visits her only briefly each evening, and in both versions, Beauty is given a magic mirror with which to entertain and distract herself during her imprisonment. The mirror functions like a window to her fantasy but also a window to her culture, an eerie prefigurement of television.

De Villeneuve's story of "Beauty and the Beast" has Beauty, sans most of her virtuous trappings, doing her duty to her father. Once trapped in her dutiful role, she must make the best of it. Beauty is lectured by the female fairy who visits her in her dreams: "Be a model of female generosity. Show yourself to be as wise as you are charming. Don't hesitate to sacrifice your passion to your duty" (Zipes 1989, p. 180).

The beast had been enchanted by the fairy. He is actually a "prince more handsome than Eros himself" and appears to Beauty in dreams (Zipes 1989, p. 244). De Villeneuve refers to her dream figure as the "handsome unknown." Beauty states to the prince, "I owe everything to the Beast. He anticipates all my wishes. I'm indebted to him for the joy of knowing you" (ibid., pp. 179–180).

What we see in this story is archetypal in the sense that it describes both the historical situation of women coping with their culture, as well as the problem of the psyche as it forms into complexes as every individual deals with the allotted culture. Culture forces us all to sacrifice our passions for our duties. In the culture current when this fairy tale was written, the demand to conform forced individuals to suppress passion and repress impulses that otherwise would have developed more fully.

Learning to love the beast, to agree to be his bride, Beauty liberates the Prince. As did the Green Knight in Gawain's quest, the beast becomes more civilized and cultivated as he becomes known. In terms of individuation, the individual must learn to differentiate the beast that drives from within and from without and to discriminate (break the enchantment) between what is useful and what is not useful in the composition of the beast.

When trauma contaminates the father complex, however, the already difficult challenge of adapting to culture becomes problematic. Trauma symptoms of avoidance and repetition charge the process of adaptation with a life-and-death urgency. Grim determination replaces creative solution. Survival replaces liberation.

The Modern Beast

The 1992 Disney version of "Beauty and the Beast" shows the nascent professional woman in Belle, yearning for books. " 'All that beauty,' the villagers would say, shaking their heads. 'It's a shame she's not normal. She always has her head buried in a book. She's just as strange as her father'" (Singer 1992, p. 5). Disney's is, of course, a corporate collective version that is remarkably different from either of the eighteenth-century French versions and from the poetic experimental 1946 version by Cocteau, which follows Leprince de Beaumont. The Disney version drops the vain, lazy sisters who tease and mock Beauty. What in the eighteenth century was competition from the feminine becomes a comical, vain, macho male suitor, Gaston. Gaston is the town hunk, and he is shunned by Beauty but yearned after by a buxom chorus of three women. The Disney paradox is that the handsome hunk is the anti-intellectual beast and the enchanted beast is presented as an empathic and caring male who is to turn into the true lover-prince at the end of the story.

Disney adds a scene from Charles Perrault's fairy tale, "Blue Beard," when Beast forbids Belle from entering the room in which the enchanted rose is wilting like a botanical clock. The corporate author also adds the requisite crowd-pleasing violent battle between the beast (the good guy) and vain, jealous Gaston.

What appears to have evolved in modern Western life is the transformation of the negative female into the negative male as the force that opposes the union of Beauty and the beast. Gaston is allied with the villagers as a male force just as the police forces were aligned against Thelma and Louise, preventing their escape. The male beast is entirely projected and the negative feminine has degenerated into a curvaceous comic triad.

The modern versions of the story of "Beauty and the Beast" are variations of an archetypal pattern. How the archetype is played out is usually unconscious for the player. In the case of the professional woman, Beatrice, mentioned earlier, who has a psychic beast complex that is generated by a dominant and traumatizing father, the trauma adds a vehement energy to the father complex. She reacts to the energy by driving herself to compete, entering a bestial world of a profession dominated by men, and working in the most prestigious and demanding institution in her city. She prevails over her peers, struggles with the institutional powers that dominate, and is considered among the top professionals in her field. She continually dreams of beasts: "I go into the parking lot and am walking to my car when a man comes up and starts to stalk me. I just barely make it to my car." "I wake up knowing that a man is in the hall about to come through my door." "A man kills another woman brutally with a knife and then starts chasing me."

As she strives to cope and prevail in her profession and in her life in the city, she fails to care sufficiently for her own well-being. She fills her vacations with dutiful visits to friends and family. She works grimly at recreation. She is a good friend to both men and women but never asks for favors. She hates dependency in any form but ironically dates a man who is stolidly passive and self-effacing. She is locked into a professional situation that demands a driven working pace. Her shadow is imaged by a famous television comedian, a bouncy histrionic blonde with long red fingernails. The abundance of energy that she used in her work, she now at mid-life finds waning, and she finds herself increasingly depressed. She confronts in therapy the problem of differentiating from her shadow the feminine energy that will allow her to grow emotionally, but this requires her to gain some alliance with the nightmare beast that will give her better control over her compulsion to work. If Beatrice's mother had shown her more power, especially if she had contested her husband's domineering abuse, Beatrice might not have had so much difficulty respecting the feminine. As it was, she had to confront the father/trauma complex herself in therapy.

Summary

The emotions of psychological trauma can become associated with any existing complex in the psyche. Here, the father is seen as the abuser. When the father is a traumatized war veteran, he might impose on his son a compulsion to fight in a literal war. If the father abuses his son, the boy is likely to see himself as a violent person. If the father abuses his daughter, she may enter a different kind of war, doing battle in a male-dominated world (however, it is unlikely that she will see herself as a violent beast, but will carry a beast who is a product of a fairy's enchantment, i.e., an unconscious product). The beast is a psychic figure for the female and a shadow ego rival for the male. When he is supercharged by trauma, however, he becomes a menace. For a woman, he becomes a driving force and for the male, a rival consumer of psychic energy (as Hyde was to Jekyll) who detracts from and competes with the ego.

If the father trauma is sexual in nature, the problem is confounded still more. In the next chapter, the problem of sexual trauma is considered, specifically the sexual trauma created by father to daughter and generally by males to girls.

Chapter

8

DONKEY SKIN

Dissociation and Self-Image in Sexual Trauma

Sexual trauma and particularly the sexual mistreatment of children has very little documentation in the Western tradition of fairy and folk tales. This is most unfortunate because under standing the problems caused by sexual abuse was, until recently, not discussed much in modern literature either.

In societies that are in touch with their cultural tradition, folk tales and fairy tales provide oral lessons that keep the people in touch with themselves and their heritage, even when they are victims of violence and terror themselves. These tales create a sense of homeostasis, to wit: there is evil in the world and not just in my life, and here is how you cope with it. Unfortunately, many of the traditional Western fairy tales were purged of their sexual content, leaving very few tales dealing with the problem of sexual mistreatment. By the time they reach print, fairy tales are often censored, with sexual references deleted or greatly compromised through inference and symbolization. Tatar (1987) documents the repeated compromises of the Brothers Grimm as they brought their works to a popular audience. The girl in "The Handless Maiden," for instance, was first reported as an incest victim with the Devil of the story initially portrayed as the evil side of the father

(Tatar 1987, p. 80). The brutality of mothers and fathers, recounted orally to other adults, became the brutal deeds of stepparents when they reached print as children's stories. One story that does survive with a straightforward incest problem is "Donkey Skin," a French story ("Peau d'Ane") which can be found in Andrew Lang's collection (1967). "Peau d'Ane" was first published by Charles Perrault in 1694 (Zipes 1989, p. 67). A somewhat Christianized version is found in the Grimms' collection, "Allerleirauh" ("Thousandfurs") (Grimm and Grimm 1972).

"Donkey Skin" has elements of many of the problems that sexual trauma presents to its survivors, particularly diffusion of personal boundaries, stigmatization, betrayal, dissociation, and repetition. In this story, the king is "much beloved by his subjects" and possesses fabulous wealth, the source of which is a donkey whose ears put out gold coins when it sleeps. The king's wife becomes terminally ill and, on her death bed, makes the king promise to remarry quickly to a woman who is "more beautiful and better formed than myself." So saying, the queen dies and the king has the surrounding lands searched for such a woman, until he realizes that the only person who possesses such beauty is his own adopted daughter, "who had lived in the palace since she was a baby." The "adopted" part of the relationship seems to me to be the thinnest of disguises, designed to make incest easier to relate. In "Allerleirauh," the girl is the natural daughter, but "grown up."

In "Donkey Skin," the girl does not want to marry her father and flees to her fairy godmother. It seems to be essential in tales of domestic sexual abuse that the other parent be an accomplice, passive, or absent in some fashion. Here, the mother dies, and in her last soliloquy unwittingly sets the stage for her daughter to be abused. In coping with the threat her father presents, the daughter enters the world of magic, seeking out her fairy godmother for advice. Magic suggests, from a Jungian perspective, the intrusion into imagination of unconscious elements, introducing tricksterish action of shape changes and wish fulfillment. To a child who is trapped by sexual abuse, fantasy becomes an escape that is easy to access. Fantasy partners, as this fairy godmother seems to be, are reliable and safe companions. One may be helpless to protect one's body from the traumatizer, but the soul is free from abuse as long as it is dissociated. Without dissociation, the soul, too, might be lost.

The problem of dissociation as a coping defense in psychological trauma, and particularly childhood sexual trauma, is well documented (Chu and Dill 1990; Frankel 1990; Ogata et al. 1990; Terr 1988; Spiegel 1984, 1986, 1988). As mentioned in chapter 1, dissociation is the preferred adaptation in terms of brain specialization. West defines a dissociative reaction as "a discernible alteration in a person's thoughts, feelings, or actions, so that for a period of time certain information is not associated or integrated with other information as it normally or logically would be" (1967 p. 890). A dissociative reaction to psychological trauma represents a spontaneous escape from the unbearable threat of the moment. Sometimes this reaction is experienced by the survivor during the time of the trauma as literally leaving the body, so that what is happening to one's body is not happening to one's self. Victims report perceiving the traumatic event happening, and then being suddenly apart, away, or above themselves and looking down on or over at the action. Opera singer Teresa Stratas gives a vivid account of watching her psychotic father bashing his bloody head against the wall at age three or four:

> The memory is so vivid it's like yesterday. I don't hear anything. There's no sound. I see this man that was for me a strange man, that person that was sometimes around but that I don't relate to, bashing his head. The next thing I know is that I'm up in a corner of the room. I see that same strange person, but a little girl standing there, too. (Malitz 1990)

The moment one is traumatized, conscious awareness is forced suddenly to expand because of the traumatic discovery of new emotion and imagery that was previously unconscious (in potential). The younger the victim, the less opportunity there is to integrate the experience, which quickly takes on a psychic life of its own as a complex, becoming tricksterish in behavior. Meier notes that "complexes probably arise in the first place when the subject encounters difficulties in the process of adapting to [and] assimilating . . . new experiences" (1984, p. 177).

In "Donkey Skin," the girl hitches up a sheep to her cart after everyone is asleep and drives off to consult her fairy godmother. The sheep, as Jung has noted, is both a sacrificial animal and a symbol of goodness, as opposed to the goat, a Dionysian symbol (1921, par. 389). The fairy godmother advises the girl to request a special dress from her father as a condition for marriage: a dress that is as blue as the sky. "It will be impossible for him to get one, so you will be quite safe'" (Lang 1967, p. 2). This turns out not to be true. The king behaves in a most unkind way and threatens his weavers and dressmakers with death if they do not make such a dress, and they produce the impossible. The scene repeats the requisite three times: the girl asks her father for a moonbeam dress and a sunshine dress before she gives him her decision. Each time, the king forces his subjects to produce the impossible object on threat of death. The last bejeweled dress, the sunshine dress, glitters brilliantly.

> When the princess saw it, she pretended that the sight hurt her eyes, and retired to her room, where she found the fairy awaiting her, very much ashamed of herself. (Lang 1967, p. 4)

Here we see the first sign of stigmatization (shame) resulting from sexual mistreatment. Why is the girl ashamed of herself when it is her father who is the malefactor? The shame stands in marked contrast to the glory of the dresses and appears to be a symptom of identification with the aggressor. Often, extreme violence shames its witnesses.

The three celestial dresses appear in other fairy stories as sources of supernatural beauty and very likely refer to the ancient triune goddess as a source of power and authority, and while they do not prevent the trauma from occurring, they aid in the recovery. In "Allerleirauh," the dresses (one each of sun, moon, and stars) are demanded by the girl of her own inspiration, without the aid of the fairy, and packed cleverly by the girl into a nutshell when she flees.

The desperate girl in "Donkey Skin" finally, on the advice of the fairy, requests that the king kill his source of wealth, his donkey that produces the gold coins (which the fairy again thought he would never do), and give her the skin before she consents to the marriage. The king in his passion delivers the order promptly.

> The poor girl, seeing no escape from the fate she dreaded, wept afresh, and tore her hair; when, suddenly the fairy stood before her.
>
> "Take heart," she said, "all will now go well! Wrap yourself in this skin, and leave the palace and go as far as you can. I will look after you. Your dresses and your jewels shall follow you underground, and if you strike the earth whenever you need anything, you will have it at once." (Lang 1967, p. 7)

The animal nature of the covering is generalized in "Allerleirauh," where the girl demands the mantle be made of patches of skin from every kind of animal in the kingdom. The imagery in "Donkey Skin" is more satisfying as a symbol because the donkey, a symbol of humble, gainful work, is the source of the king's wealth. That sexual predators will sacrifice all, including wealth and status, for their compulsions is no news to clinicians or prosecutors. As Jung repeatedly tells us, when one is possessed by a complex, one's consciousness becomes shallow, one loses perspective, and one's intelligence is diminished.

The girl then becomes Donkey Skin and wanders into foreign lands until she gets a lowly job as a scullery maid and livestock tender in another kingdom. Remarkably, she is aided in her escape from her father's searchers when her fairy godmother makes her invisible. (It is a wish, no doubt, of many victims of domestic abuse that they become invisible.) Allerleirauh, on her journey, climbs into a hollow tree in order to sleep, where she is discovered by a huntsman of the king "to whom the forest belonged." When discovered she pleads, "'I am a poor child, deserted by father and mother; have pity on me, and take me with you'" (Grimm and Grimm 1967, p. 328).

Trauma Avoidance

In their animal skins, these girls, who are victims of sexual mistreatment, view themselves as ugly and disgusting, much like the war veteran in "Bearskin." Donkey Skin is the subject of ridicule until she proves herself by her diligence and hard work. Then one day, finally, she sees herself in a stream.

> Her hair and part of her face was quite concealed by the ass's head, which was drawn right over like a hood, and the filthy matted skin covered her whole body. It was the first time she had seen herself as other people saw her, and she was filled with shame at the spectacle. (Lang 1967, p. 8)

With dissociation from psychological trauma comes the neglect of the person who was abused. There follows, quite literally, identification with the aggressor. In moralistic terms, the victim becomes filthy and perceives herself and her body with shame. The craziness and evil that have happened to her and that she has witnessed become a part of her identity. As one of the king's attendants remarks: "'Donkey Skin is, next to the wolf, the most disgusting creature on the face of the earth.'" The survivor of sexual abuse, whose boundaries have been violated, attempts to establish makeshift barriers between herself and the world. She may neglect her self-care and gain weight to become unkempt and obese. She may strive to become unattractive and sexually unwanted, developing skin disorders. She may view herself as stupid and may become, because of hyperarousal and depression, an inattentive student and discipline problem. She may adopt an angry persona of tatoos, leather, spikes, and bizarre hairstyles as an expression of Donkey Skin. Yet underneath, however vaguely, she knows she is a beautiful princess—and has been set up for the prince. In modern situations of sexual trauma, the animal skin is a numb glove of emotional anesthesia (Terr 1990a and b).

This process is explained in psychodynamic language by Jung in terms of the trauma complex described in chapter 1, which contains imagery and emotional memory of abuse, being dissociated from ego identity. The ego complex loses energy, with the consequent loss of self-esteem, while the trauma complex gains power. At the same time, there is a memory of the pretrauma condition (the princess) that once approached wholeness. The beauty, with the celestial dresses, has gone underground in a hard nutshell.

Trauma Repetition

Terr (1990a and b) describes the thick skin of emotional isolation that is depicted in the works of Virginia Woolf as Woolf's own incest avoidance. In this ironic sense, her avoidance (as seen in the isolation experienced by her characters) is a repetition of her traumas.

A still more difficult problem of childhood sexual abuse is that sexuality becomes associated with the trauma complex. The two principle groups of symptoms associated with post-traumatic stress disorder are avoidance and repetition. Contents of the trauma complex intrude and fascinate at unpredictable moments. The victim of rape or incest may spend her life avoiding sexual encounters, except that periodically she will act as if possessed and behave in ways that lead her directly into revictimization. The prince of the fairy tale is a psychic denizen of the survivor and is projected onto whoever serves to help her meet her needs. Thus, the victim of sexual trauma becomes the prey again when she misperceives the intentions of her helpers. Later, perhaps in treatment, when she is not possessed and diminished in consciousness, she often expresses chagrin regarding her poor judgment. Jung states:

> Hence, unless we prefer to be made fools of by our illusions, we shall, by carefully analyzing every fascination, extract from it a portion of our own personality, like a quintessence, and slowly come to recognize that we meet ourselves time and again in a thousand disguises on the path of life. (1946, par. 534)

As in the next chapter, when Little Red Riding Hood meets the wolf and Bluebeard meets his bride, the animus becomes ominous when contaminated by the aggressor.

This is played out in "Donkey Skin" when the prince of the kingdom happens upon the farmhouse of the girl, peeps through a keyhole, and sees the girl in her room, clad in her "dress of sunshine." (For a variation of this scene, see the excerpt from "Goosegirl at the Well," in chapter 2.) Then the story awkwardly states that the girl knew the prince was looking at her surreptitiously. The prince grows ill with feverish love for the girl, finds out her name, and asks for a cake made by the "disgusting" Donkey Skin. The story then relates:

> But whether she had actually seen him or only heard him spoken of, directly she received the queen's command, she flung off the dirty skin, washed herself from head to foot, and put on a skirt and bodice of shining silver. Then, locking herself into her room, she took the richest cream, the finest flour, and the freshest eggs on the farm, and set about making her cake. (Lang 1967, p. 11)

Allerleirauh makes the king a bread soup that is the best he has ever tasted. She makes short, tentative appearances at the king's festive gatherings in her celestial dresses, only to slip away and return to her bestial disguise. (The male version of this pattern is played out when the hero on a feeble horse changes into his glittering armor, enters the hopeless battle anonymously, and wins the battle for the king on three consecutive days.) This repeating transition from the beautiful into the bestial and back reflects the trickster nature of the borderline state between conscious and unconscious in which neither complex has sufficient energy to sustain dominance.

The third time she serves the soup, the girl slips her magic ring, a symbol of the union of opposites, into the soup, and the king discovers her identity when she fails to return fully to her disguise, leaving her ring finger exposed (i.e., not covered with filth). In "Donkey Skin," the girl slips her ring into the cake, and the prince, when he eats the cake, discovers it and asks his parents, who are anxious about his recovery, for the bride who fits the ring. (Recall in "Bearskin" that the war veteran slips a ring half into the glass of his betrothed.) The prince's parents then have the land searched, and, in a Cinderella ritual, every female in the kingdom attempts to fit the ring to her finger before Donkey Skin is given a try.

> The ring slipped on with the utmost ease, and, as it did so, the [donkey] skin fell to the ground, disclosing a figure of such beauty that the prince, weak as he was, fell on his knees before her, while the king and queen joined their prayers to his. (Lang 1967, p. 14)

Note the very strong suggestion in the last line that the girl in her full glory is indeed a goddess. The archetypal template of the goddess in humble attire is Demeter in grief and mourning for her abducted daughter, Persephone (Homer 1976, p. 7). The making of cakes and bread soup reinforces this divine association to the goddess of grain and harvest. Persephone, abducted and ravaged by the lord of the underworld (Hades/Dionysus), becomes the symbol of lost innocence and the tie to the underworld to which she is forced annually to return.

The prince or king, as a psychic image living in the survivor, the creative animus, performs the same function as the youngest daughter of the merchant in "Bearskin," which is a male version of the recovery problem presented by psychological trauma. The animus represents the healing, creative, active factor in the survivor's recovery. However, as important as helpers are in the recovery of trauma survivors, it is a mistake for the survivor to project onto such persons the images of the princely animus. As many tellers of fairy tales have warned, too often predators come disguised or misperceived as princes. It is the problem of the trauma survivor that when the trauma complex is activated by external cues, hyperarousal from the midbrain signals the cortex, and the survivor consequently focuses on the object, becoming interested in and even fascinated by the projection. Thus, the survivor of sexual mistreatment can be retraumatized because she falls in love (becomes infatuated) with someone who elicits trauma cues, often because the predator also has a history of psychological trauma that the survivor unconsciously observes. The currently popular term *co-dependency* suggests this mutual unconscious attraction between survivors of psychological traumas. Often the hook that elicits the "prince" projection is the impression that there is something good that can be saved in the person, e.g., he is a hidden prince with great potential.

There is a similarity in these tales of incest to "Cinderella." The parallels are in the degradation of self-esteem, the loss of mother who is replaced by a fairy, the glorious dresses, and especially the process of the search and fitting. Tatar notes that seventy-seven versions of "Cinderella" have "unnatural" fathers (a Victorian euphemism for incestuous) (1987, p. 153). She also observes that there has been an evolution in fairy tales of the problem of the predatory father and jealous mother that has led to the separation of these stories, in some of which the father atrophies into virtual nonexistence and the stepmother is left as the sole active parent and the jealous villain, or the father is the obvious villain and the mother diminishes (ibid., p. 150).

PTSD in the Adult Traumatized as a Child

Survivors of child abuse are unconsciously likely to carry their trauma symptoms into adulthood. Terr (1981, 1990a) reported her observation that children will "play" trauma games after they have themselves survived a psychological trauma. The word *play* is qualified with quotation marks because the children do not usually derive pleasure from the games. Trauma play is not fun for the survivor, rather it is compulsive and repetitious, but it tends to be adopted by other children, who do have fun. Tartar notes horrible examples in folk tales of children playing butcher with each other, which the Grimms subsequently dropped from their collection (1987, p. 198). Trauma games are quite likely rituals enacted during periods of traumatic reexperiencing, such as van der Kolk (1989) described. Thus, a girl who is raped at age five while playing a game of hide-and-seek with older kids may at age thirteen be raped again while playing a sexual game. A crass observer, often the rapist himself, may say that "she asked for it" by her behavior. Moralists may assert that she "deserved what she got." Uninformed observers, however, do not realize that the survivor of sexual trauma is acting under a dissociated (hypnotic) state and that her "play" is conducted with diminished consciousness.

Children who are traumatically disciplined may subsequently "play" at punishment, and in their play often elicit further traumas. Marcus (1985) describes flagellation pornography in mid-Victorian England as a compulsion to repeat the public school floggings, which could be considered a form of posttraumatic play. Marcus observes that literary pornography's most "striking quality" is the compulsion to repeat endlessly (ibid., p. 279).

The children who are sexually mistreated and adults who were sexually mistreated as children will, during these periods of posttraumatic play, be unconscious of the sexual/traumatic consequences of their behaviors or only vaguely aware, as spectators dissociated from the action. The trauma complex, when activated, pushes aside the ego complex that would, in its wisdom, not conduct the survivor's behavior in a way that leads to retraumatization. Jung states:

> An active complex puts us momentarily under a state of duress of compulsive thinking and acting, for which under certain conditions the only appropriate term would be the judicial concept of diminished responsibility. (1948c, par. 200)

These holes in consciousness in which one behaves compulsively and not in one's own best interests present a sensitive problem socially. This is one way victims get blamed for the traumas, and it is how predators, as Jung implies, defend themselves in court. Feminists and those who advocate for victims object to the idea that a woman could behave unconsciously in a sexual fashion. But the symptoms of psychological trauma are periodically unconsciously "played out" by the survivor, unless he or she is given treatment and education regarding the nature of PTSD to generate sufficient insight to spot the behavior as it begins to occur.

Posttraumatic play is not like a flashback but is a repetition phenomenon of trauma reenactment. The survivor's identity acts as an observer of the action, often with the same kind of comment an uninvolved observer might make, to the effect of "Oh, oh, this is foolish, I shouldn't be doing this." By contrast, the flashback is usually followed by amnesia and involves the literal reenactment of a traumatic scene. (Terr (1990a) observes that children do not usually have flashbacks.) In a flashback, the survivor is out of touch with the present and very often has experienced a loss of conscious functioning, with the trauma imagery superimposed on the perception of the present like an overlaid map.

A third kind of reexperiencing occurs when the survivor is perfectly relaxed and off guard, at which time a trauma cue is encountered that causes a loss of consciousness with the intrusion of a trauma memory but no acting out of the trauma. For example, one combat veteran reported driving on a lovely day, fully relaxed, when he came upon an accident scene with emergency vehicles in attendance. He went into a trance, recalling a Vietnam medical evacuation scene involving his wounded friend, which lasted until a policeman woke him and told him to move on.

Trauma reenactment can also be seen in adults who are survivors of psychological trauma when they react to present events in a manner that is appropriate for the trauma circumstances. For example, the survivor of childhood sexual trauma responds passively to demands made upon her, misperceiving her power to affect her present condition. As the wicked witch said, in *The Wizard of Oz*, "I can sill make her my slave, for she does not know how to use her power" (Baum 1900, p. 150). Behaving as though the trauma were recurring affects the survivor even in sexual circumstances that are desirable, when she knows that she is choosing her partner and wants the encounter. The body may respond negatively in spite of the wishes of the ego. A trauma complex unfortunately cannot be willed away. One client described her feet turning into her boyfriend's workplace, even after he had beaten her nearly to death, turning in against her will as though her shoes were directing her.

Fate and Fantasy in the Trauma Survivor

There is a persistent sense of fate that affects the sense of future motivation of survivors, particularly if they have been traumatized repeatedly. Having been overwhelmed by events alters the locus of control so that cues reinforce the trauma experience. For example, a shop owner exploits an employee by pressuring her to work overtime, and she capitulates. As a survivor of multiple traumas, she is prone to state that she is fated to encounter people who take advantage of her. To her, this is a powerful argument because the pressure from her employer recalls in her the trauma emotions and reinforces her view that she is helpless, ultimately, to control her life. Upon analysis, it is apparent that she avoids men, except those who approach her, a process that selects for dominating males. Neiderland (1984) alludes to a belief in fate held by concentration camp survivors who are compulsive gamblers. Terr (1983) speculates that the distortion of time sense in trauma may play a role in the perception of fate, when the survivors review the events preceding the trauma as omens of what is to come, reinforcing their belief in fate.

Fantasy often plays a part in trauma reenactment. Psychological trauma causes an expansion of consciousness. Although it is unwanted consciousness, the accessible repertoire of the mind is expanded. The traumatic expansion of consciousness may quickly be blocked, compartmentalized, and the mind constricted. In other cases, fantasy may be a creative adaptation, as in the case of the more plastic and flexible child, such as exemplified earlier by Robert Louis Stevenson (see chapter 5). Trauma fantasy may be the logical adult extension of trauma play in children.

The trauma survivor doesn't necessarily use the trauma directly incorporated into fantasy, but the psychological trauma event is so highly charged with energy that it gives the trauma imagery and even accidental associations a powerful fascination. What is acted out in play in a child age five is more likely to be acted out in fantasy by a child age twelve. Compulsive sexual fantasy in adults, the sort that we see leading to sexual acting out, often has as its origin the sexual trauma in the child. Marcus (1985), influenced by Freud, notes that pornography, which has the repetition compulsion as its characteristic, probably has its origins in adolescent sexual experience. This is particularly true when sexual trauma involves premature sexual stimulation. The first sexual stimulation to orgasm can be the genesis of an emotional experience that becomes a salient complex when it cannot be integrated into the ego complex, regardless of whether or not it is traumatic. Whether or not the sexual fantasy is acted upon depends on the level of ego strength, i.e., the grounding of the individual in the present. As a supplement to reality, sexual fantasy may be satisfying and useful; however, when fantasy replaces or is mistaken for reality, it can be destructive or at least foolish. Indulging sexual fantasy such that it becomes a mushrooming habit that vies with ego or even forms its own ego is a problem discussed earlier in chapter 5. Certainly, trauma-based fantasy can quickly become intrusive and compulsive until it is understood and processed creatively.

Summary

Dissociation is a common way that children cope with sexual mistreatment. Stigmatization is inflicted on the survivor of sexual abuse and results in diminished self-esteem and a stunting of emotional growth. Compulsion to repeat the traumatic experience takes many forms that are often subtle. For children, the repetition compulsion will often take the form of posttraumatic play and for adults play becomes sexual fantasy. Even after successful treatment, the survivor of sexual trauma doesn't cease to associate sex to whatever is randomly associated to the trauma at the time. The advantage that clinical treatment can offer is that when the survivor experiences the trauma memories and an intrusion of fascination relating to the trauma experience, she or he does not have to act on the experience in a way that is self-destructive. For instance, instead of compulsively accepting a ride from the man who says that she is beautiful, a woman with PTSD can learn to reflect on the invitation as her trauma complex is cued, recognize her reaction, and stop the reexperiencing before she acts as if she were fated to comply. Repetition of the trauma need not be entirely negative but can also lead to new insights and psychological growth.

The emotional numbing that results from coping with repetitive trauma creates a thick skin of defensive boundaries. When the trauma complex breaks through into consciousness unintegrated, the boundary skin falls away and the survivor is again unprotected and vulnerable. However, when treatment can help the survivor integrate the trauma complex, she or he can experience the dropping away of the ugly skin and yet remain protected by the expanded consciousness that accepts the sexual trauma with all the other facts in life, neither hiding it nor hiding within it.

Fairy tales, myths, legends, and creations of our contemporary culture are expressions of human problems, and psychological traumas present the greatest of human problems to be mastered. In the next chapter, "Living with Death," adaptation in the face of trauma is discussed in more detail.

Chapter

9

"As I travel into the world of psychic trauma, I begin to perceive more and more universal, societal, cultural, and individual effects which have originated in overwhelming external events."
Terr, *Too Scared to Cry*

LIVING WITH DEATH

Resilience and the "Markers of Disobedience"

It is true for all the classes of trauma described in chapter 1, at whatever intensity, that the survivor has felt the threat of death. It may be that in some kinds of sexual trauma, death *per se* is not the threat, but when the victim is overwhelmed and forced to submit, death is arguably present as an insult to identity. Trauma leaves the survivor with a new awareness and, in effect, causes the innocent pretrauma identity to coexist with the bestial trauma identity. At best, the survivor of trauma is mature and able to make a conscious observation that what follows from psychological trauma (the symptoms of PTSD and its variations) is natural and as old as humanity. More often, however, the survivor is unconscious of the consequences of trauma, and some variation of an ambivalent,

Jekyll-and-Hyde relationship results between pretrauma and posttrauma identities.

There are many fairy tales that illustrate this problem, which is most often portrayed as an innocent meeting a beast and being physically devoured or threatened with dismemberment. Two prominent fairy-tale versions of this motif are "Little Red Riding Hood" and "Blue Beard" ("Barbe Bleue") in Perrault's 1697 collection (Zipes 1989).

It is essential in understanding these fairy tales that we not assert that because the protagonist is female these are gender-specific stories. Rather, "Little Red Riding Hood" and "Blue Beard" operate on two levels. They present the problem that girls face when they leave home, usually to marry, and they present the universal human problem of seeking to explore the world, in which "brutal nature," as Robert Louis Stevenson observed, soon intervenes.

Wolf as Death

The best illustration of the problem comes to us in the oral rendering of "Little Red Riding Hood" as presented by Dundes (1989 p. 198), a version predating Perrault's. In the oral tradition, the girl is given food to take to her grandmother by her mother. She is intercepted in the woods by the wolf, who asks her which road she will take: the road of pins or the road of needles. She chooses the road of pins, the easier road for anyone who has to sew. The wolf quickly precedes Little Red Riding Hood to the grandmother's, chops up the old woman, and places her meat and blood in the pantry. He then dons grandmother's bedclothes. When Little Red Riding Hood arrives, she gives the wolf the food, and he invites her to partake of the repast in the pantry—which she does. He then invites Little Red Riding Hood to remove her clothes and come to bed with him. Little Red Riding Hood innocently undresses:

> When she asks where to put her apron, bodice, dress, petticoat, and long stockings, the wolf replies each time with "Throw them into the fire, my child, you won't be needing them any more." (Dundes 1989, p. 198)

Little Red Riding Hood climbs into bed with the wolf and remarks about her grandmother's odd appearance in a repetitive manner until she finally realizes the danger she is in and cleverly asks to be excused to relieve herself outside. The wolf urges her to "do it" in bed, but she wheedles her way outside tied to a string, undoes the string, and runs to safety.

In Perrault's version, she is killed and devoured. In the Grimms' two versions, she is either devoured and then rescued by the hunter, who kills the wolf, or she engineers the death of the wolf when he falls into a cooking pot, in "The Three Little Pigs" style.

When psychologically traumatized, the survivor is presented with a new identity that must incorporate death. The wolf represented death to the peasant population that formed an audience for the oral version of "Little Red Riding Hood"—natural death or psychic death. In some versions, he is a werewolf. Eventually every mother must send her children out to face death. To keep them home would represent a loss of their own individuality. To interpret this action otherwise would be incongruous; a mother would not send her daughter out alone through woods populated by wolves. This is not a story of trauma from the mother, but it is certainly about the traumas that life presents. Little Red Riding Hood is duped into eating the flesh and blood of her grandmother. A Jungian approach would have it that the grandmother really is a grandmother whose time has come, and the wolf is nature's agent. The death of a grandparent is the most common touchstone of death for a child. Some lose their siblings or parents, some have their own encounters with death, but most will lose their grandparents in childhood, especially those children from the cultures that created the oral version of this story. Bettelheim points to the parallel myth of the ancient god, Chronos, who eats his children (1989b, p. 189). What is immediately present when we are traumatized is natural, and death will devour us if we let it. The child who "eats" her grandmother incorporates her consciousness. Being near death deepens consciousness, making it wider and darker.

The sexual aspect of "Little Red Riding Hood" is highlighted in Perrault and downplayed in the Grimms' version.

Why on earth can't the child see through the wolf's disguise? It must be a magic wolf, enchanted, as was Death, the lord of the castle, in "Sir Gawain and the Green Knight." The child being seduced by the wolf was a source of satiric moralizing by Perrault: "Gentle wolves are of all such creatures the most dangerous!" (1989, p. 6). We must appreciate that, for the peasant who shared the oral version of this tale, childhood as a state separate from mother did not exist; one was either attached to mother's apron strings or one was a working adult. The sexual overtones of "Little Red Riding Hood" dramatically illustrate the brutal transition from childhood to adulthood without adolescence. The Vietnam veteran saw death at age eighteen and nineteen in combat, but the child sees death in the form of psychological trauma suddenly, often repeatedly, with incommunicable emotions.

Crucial to understanding "Little Red Riding Hood" is the oral rendition of the girl's escape. Recall Jung's quotation: "*in stercore invenitur*" ("It is found in filth"). (The Lone Ranger would say, "It is found in wild silver.") The girl flees the wolf by feigning the call to nature. She becomes the trickster (e.g., the culture hero Raven/Hermes). Tartar refers to the "markers of disobedience" that highlight fairy tales of resilience and survival (1987, p. 46). Hermes is the Greek god of adaptation. As trickster and cultural hero in one, he is the god of the borderline state, the god of the crossroads, of commerce, of dealing with strangers, and of thievery and magic. He is the god of clever children. One cannot avoid, it seems, wolf/nature, but the survivor of trauma has at his or her disposal the raw material for adaptation and readjustment—which is the trickster energy that is generated by the dynamics of the state of flux and change created by the trauma itself. Some survivors of early childhood traumas develop a perpetual borderline state of adolescent mutability that is marked by brief psychotic episodes and is currently labeled "borderline personality disorder." Little Red Riding Hood is able to escape the wolf by deception but, when traumas become redundant, the originally adaptive role of trickster becomes a personality style.

Blue Beard the Batterer

In "Blue Beard," we get a sense of the form the trauma may take for the girl when she leaves her mother. Blue Beard is a wealthy man who is disliked because of (among other things) the color of his beard. He has taken many wives but they have all disappeared. He seeks to marry one of two beautiful daughters and wins one of them by being generous to her friends and family. When she goes to live with him, he is called away on business and gives her the keys to the mansion. He tells her that she can go into any room, except "the little room at the end of a long corridor on the ground floor." When Blue Beard leaves, the woman's friends arrive and explore his fabulous wealth. His wife immediately runs downstairs to open the forbidden door. There she discovers a carnary containing the dismembered corpses of his previous wives. The frightened woman drops the key, and it becomes stained with blood. When Blue Beard returns, he quickly discovers her deed and threatens to kill her with his sword. She begs to have time to make her peace with God. She then calls to her sister to go up in the tower and look out for her brothers who are en route on a visit to her. She calls out to her sister three times: "Anne! Sister Anne! Do you see anyone coming?" and the third time, Anne reports that her brothers are riding up and signals them to hurry. They arrive, slay Blue Beard, and his widow inherits his wealth.

"Blue Beard" is a common fairy-tale motif of the murderous husband and gives us a sense of one of the forms that death took for girls of a marriagable age. In a very ancient Greek version, Blue Beard is death himself who devours girls who refuse to eat his fare. In other versions, Blue Beard slays three sisters, one following the other, with the last sometimes surviving and freeing the others by returning them to life (Leach 1972, p. 150).

Perrault's version presents a persevering female, similar to the resilient Little Red Riding Hood, who escapes death's clutches by not giving up. In a psychodynamic model, the captive wife dissociates, splits her consciousness, with one part being "Sister Anne" dispatched to the tower to watch for help.

Then she is rescued by the adaptive, masculine energy in the form of the brothers, which renders her active enough to break away from death. Momentarily dissociating saves her from being totally overwhelmed.

Trauma Imagery as Carnage

Persons who are traumatized readily imagine that more traumas are going to follow. For this reason, they have difficulty imagining the future. I recently had as a client a young woman who was the survivor of many (mostly sexual) traumas dating back to a very early age. She had been living with a group of friends who borrowed money from her, abused alcohol, and were undependable. When we discussed the possibility of her getting her own room in a boarding house, she stated that she was afraid and imagined the person who ran the house would be a "psycho," referring to the Alfred Hitchcock horror movie about the killer who ran a motel. She knew just how bad her friends were, but any new situation presented an ambiguous mix of the known and the unknown which allowed her trauma-fed imagination to play at projection. I suggested that perhaps she could evaluate the risk and described a hypothetical low-risk "little old landlady." Then, she said, she could imagine a little old lady with a basement full of bodies.

Perrault, in his clever moral rhymes at the end of "Blue Beard," suggests that the fairy tale is about women's sexual curiosity:

> With all due respect, ladies, the thrill is slight
> For as soon as you're satisfied, it goes away.

and about spousal battering:

> No longer are husbands so terrible. (Zipes 1989, p. 35)

Carnage and carnal knowledge have the same root—*carne*—flesh; the former refers to disunion, the latter to sexual union.

One could also argue that "Blue Beard" is addressing the

same theme as "Little Red Riding Hood," to wit: these are stories about psychological trauma as it was commonly experienced by girls who came of age and left home, and that the stories are also about the innocent but resilient psyche, the consciousness that encounters the overwhelming threat of death and survives.

Lenore Terr has written extensively about the problems presented by the repetition symptoms of PTSD, and particularly about the dynamics of trauma in the imagination of the survivor. She notes that traumas of early childhood, prior to thirty-six months of age, are usually not recovered in the eidetic memory at all, but that behavioral (body) memory occurs with even much earlier trauma (1988). The difference in memory is between the looping memory of primary consciousness (body memory) and the long-term eidetic memory produced after the hippocampus is fully developed (about age two). Terr observes that writers such as Stephen King, who were traumatized as children, extend a form of childhood trauma play in their creative works as adults (1989b, 1990a). I see my aforementioned client traumas projected not so very playfully into an ambiguous situation imagined in the future. One of the reasons that the survivors of psychological trauma have little or no sense of future and prefer to live day by day is that imagining the future forces them to project onto a blank screen that stimulates the trauma complex. Whitmont, discussing unconscious complexes, observes that "we may be attracted by something which 'wants to be known . . .'" (1969, p. 61). In that sense, trauma symptoms like intrusive recollection and trauma play are healthy impulses toward wholeness. Recall Jung's comment that

> a complex can be really overcome only if it is lived out to the full. In other words, if we are to develop further we have to draw to us and drink down to the very dregs what, because of our complexes, we have held at a distance. (1935, par. 184)

Lenore Terr asserts, however, that the trauma play she observes in children and writers is not healing but compulsively repetitious without development. This is where the analyst and psychotherapist are crucial in the role of breaking the survivor out of the repetition cycle with interpretation and suggestion. Behavioral techniques such as eye movement desensitization (Shapiro 1989) may create synaptic change in the visual center of the brain, interrupting the repeating dream or intrusive memory, and perhaps creating the synaptic changes necessary for reintegration of the trauma. But it is the trauma survivor, in the end, who must face death again in the form of the trauma complex, repeatedly, without giving up, keeping one part of the conscious psyche alert for signs of strength to overcome and integrate the complex. By voluntarily dissociating from the trauma complex, the survivor is able to watch its action and choose to act or not act in response.

Summary

The reason that trauma disorder has only recently been discussed as a problem (mainly in this last century) is not because it is more common now, but rather because it has only recently become *uncommon* enough to be considered beyond the norm. In previous centuries, I would conjecture, it was uncommon for someone to survive without psychological trauma. War, pestilence, plague, child abuse, sexual abuse, spousal battering, slavery, predatory exploitation of children, peasants, and workers, life-threatening accidents, infections that are now easily treated with antibiotics, overwhelmingly painful medical procedures, high infant mortality, and high mother mortality all led to a life expectancy below what we now consider middle age (Herlihy 1978). It has only been in this century, in the past fifty years, that someone could reasonably hope to live a life without psychological trauma.

Those who are now unlucky enough to incur psychological trauma, who have to lie down with the wolf from time to time, may have to cooperate and submit to fate. However, as survivors, who are at war with the collective and at war even with themselves, to conform to fate after the trauma is to suppress the trauma identity and compromise individuality. To properly integrate the unwanted trauma consciousness, the survivor must consciously carry the trauma identity while traveling a unique path to recovery with no collective markers.

References

Anand, K. J. S., and Hickey, P. R. 1992. Halothane-morphine compared with high dose subentanil for anesthesia and postoperative analgesia in neonatal cardiac surgery. *New England Journal of Medicine* 326(1):1–9.

Baum, L. Frank. 1900. *The Wonderful Wizard of Oz.* New York: Dover Publications, 1960.

Beck, J. C., and van der Kolk, B. 1987. Reports of childhood incest and current behavior of chronically hospitalized psychotic women. *American Journal of Psychiatry* 144(11):1474–1476.

Benedikt, R. A., and Kolb, L. C. 1986. Preliminary findings on chronic pain and posttraumatic stress disorder. *American Journal of Psychiatry* 143(7):908–910.

Bergman, Ingmar. 1960. *The Seventh Seal.* In *Four Screenplays by Ingmar Bergman,* L. Malmstrom and D. Kushner, trans. New York: Simon and Schuster.

Bettelheim, Bruno. 1979. *Surviving.* New York: Knopf.

. 1989a. *The Uses of Enchantment.* New York: Vintage Books.

_____. 1989b. Little red cap and the pubertal girl. In *Little Red Riding Hood: A Casebook,* Alan Dundes, ed. Madison, Wisc.: University of Wisconsin Press, pp. 168–192.

Bolen, Jean S. 1984. *Goddesses in Everywoman.* New York: Harper and Row.

Bowlby, John. 1979. *The Making and Breaking of Affectional Bonds.* London: Tavistock Publications.

_____. 1988. Developmental psychiatry comes of age. *American Journal of Psychiatry* 145(1):1–10.

Calder, Jenni. 1980. *Robert Louis Stevenson: A Life Story.* London: Oxford University Press.

Carmen, E., Rieker, P., and Mills, T. 1984. Victims of violence and psychiatric illness. *American Journal of Psychiatry* 141:378–383.

Cavenar, J. O., Nash, J. L., and Maltbie, A. A. 1978. Anniversary reactions presenting as physical complaints. *Journal of Clinical Psychiatry* 39(4):369–374.

Cazzaniga, M. S. 1989. Organization of the human brain. *Science* 245:947–952.

Chu, J. A., and Dill, D. L. 1990. Dissociative symptoms in relation to childhood and sexual abuse. *American Journal of Psychiatry* 147(7):887–892.

Daiches, David. 1973. *Robert Louis Stevenson and His World.* London: Thames and Hudson.

Damlouji, N. F., and Ferguson, J. M. 1985. Three cases of posttraumatic anorexia nervosa. *American Journal of Psychiatry* 142(3):362–363.

Danieli, Yael. 1985. The treatment and prevention of long-term effects and intergenerational transmission of victimization: A lesson from Holocaust survivors and their children. In *Trauma and Its Wake,* C. R. Figley, ed. New York: Brunner/Mazel, pp. 295–313.

Demetrapoulas, S. A. 1979. Hestia, goddess of the hearth: Notes on an oppressed archetype. *Spring,* pp. 55–75.

deWind, E. 1968. The confrontation with death. *International Journal of Psychoanalysis* 49:302–374.

Dundes, A. 1989. Interpreting "Little Red Riding Hood" psychoanalytically. In *Little Red Riding Hood: A Casebook*, A. Dundes, ed. Madison, Wisc.: The University of Wisconsin Press, pp. 193–238.

Durning, J. 1976. *Tune in Yesterday.* Englewood Cliffs, N.J.: Prentice Hall.

Edelman, G. M. 1992. *Bright Air, Brilliant Fire: On the Matter of the Mind.* New York: Basic Books.

Epstein, Helen. 1981. *Children of the Holocaust.* New York: Bantam.

Frankel, F. H. 1990. Hypnotizability and dissociation. *American Journal of Psychiatry* 147(7):823–829.

Gantz, J., trans. 1976. *Mabinogion.* New York: Penguin Books.

Gies, Frances, and Gies, Joseph. 1987. *Marriage and the Family in the Middle Ages.* New York: Harper and Row.

Glassman, J., Magulac, M., and Darko, D. 1987. Folie a famille: Shared paranoid disorder in a Vietnam veteran and his family. *American Journal of Psychiatry* 144(5):658–660.

Goethe, Johann Wolfgang. 1983. *Faust*, Phillip Wayne, trans. New York: Penguin Books.

Gould, Stephen J. 1991. Eight (or fewer) little piggies. *Natural History* (January), pp. 22–29.

Graves, R. 1948. *The White Goddess.* London: Farrar, Straus, Giroux.

_____ 1951. *Goodbye and All That.* New York: Doubleday.

Greenspan, G. S., and Samuel, S. E. 1989. Self-cutting after rape. *American Journal of Psychiatry* 146(7):789–790.

Grimm, J., and Grimm, W. 1972. *The Complete Grimms' Fairy Tales,* M. Hunt and J. Stern, trans. New York: Pantheon Books.

Heinrich, B. 1989. *Ravens in Winter.* New York: Summit Books.

Henderson, Joseph L. 1967. *Thresholds of Initiation.* Middletown, Conn.: Wesleyan University Press.

Hennessy, James Pope. 1974. *Robert Louis Stevenson.* New York: Simon and Schuster.

Herlihy, D. 1978. The natural history of medieval women. *Natural History* 87(3):56–67.

Hilgard, E., and Bower, G. *Theories of Learning.* New York: Apple-ton-Century-Crofts.

Homer. 1937. *The Odyssey,* W. H. D. Rouse, trans. New York: New American Library.

_____. 1976. *The Homeric Hymns,* A. N. Athaussakis, trans. Baltimore: Johns Hopkins University Press.

Jung, C. G. 1907. The feeling-toned complex and its general effects on the psyche. In *CW* 3:38–51. Princeton, N.J.: Princeton University Press, 1972.

_____. 1921. *Psychological Types. CW,* vol. 6. Princeton, N.J.: Princeton University Press, 1971.

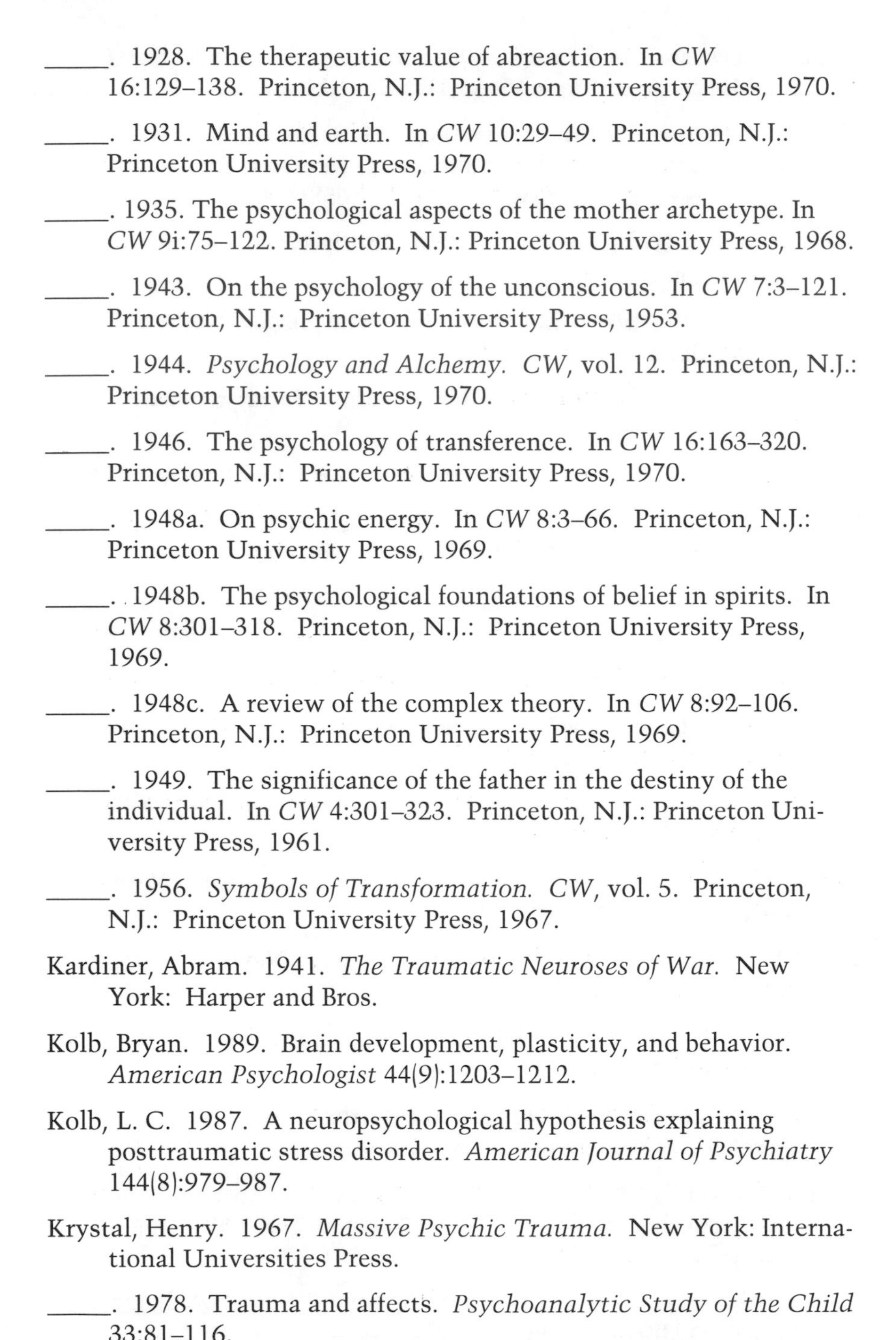

_____. 1928. The therapeutic value of abreaction. In *CW* 16:129–138. Princeton, N.J.: Princeton University Press, 1970.

_____. 1931. Mind and earth. In *CW* 10:29–49. Princeton, N.J.: Princeton University Press, 1970.

_____. 1935. The psychological aspects of the mother archetype. In *CW* 9i:75–122. Princeton, N.J.: Princeton University Press, 1968.

_____. 1943. On the psychology of the unconscious. In *CW* 7:3–121. Princeton, N.J.: Princeton University Press, 1953.

_____. 1944. *Psychology and Alchemy*. *CW*, vol. 12. Princeton, N.J.: Princeton University Press, 1970.

_____. 1946. The psychology of transference. In *CW* 16:163–320. Princeton, N.J.: Princeton University Press, 1970.

_____. 1948a. On psychic energy. In *CW* 8:3–66. Princeton, N.J.: Princeton University Press, 1969.

_____. 1948b. The psychological foundations of belief in spirits. In *CW* 8:301–318. Princeton, N.J.: Princeton University Press, 1969.

_____. 1948c. A review of the complex theory. In *CW* 8:92–106. Princeton, N.J.: Princeton University Press, 1969.

_____. 1949. The significance of the father in the destiny of the individual. In *CW* 4:301–323. Princeton, N.J.: Princeton University Press, 1961.

_____. 1956. *Symbols of Transformation*. *CW*, vol. 5. Princeton, N.J.: Princeton University Press, 1967.

Kardiner, Abram. 1941. *The Traumatic Neuroses of War*. New York: Harper and Bros.

Kolb, Bryan. 1989. Brain development, plasticity, and behavior. *American Psychologist* 44(9):1203–1212.

Kolb, L. C. 1987. A neuropsychological hypothesis explaining posttraumatic stress disorder. *American Journal of Psychiatry* 144(8):979–987.

Krystal, Henry. 1967. *Massive Psychic Trauma*. New York: International Universities Press.

_____. 1978. Trauma and affects. *Psychoanalytic Study of the Child* 33:81–116.

_____. 1988. *Integration and Self Healing: Affect, Trauma, Alexithymia.* New York: Analytic Press.

Lang, A., ed. 1966. *The Violet Fairy Book.* New York: Dover.

_____. 1967. *The Grey Fairy Book.* New York: Dover.

Leach, Maria, ed. 1972. *Funk and Wagnalls Standard Dictionary of Folklore, Mythology, and Legend.* New York: Harper and Row.

Levy, David. 1945. Psychic trauma of operations in children. *American Journal of the Diseases of Children* 69:7–25.

Malitz, Nancy. 1990. The lady sometimes vanishes. *The New York Times Magazine*, February 26, pp. 24–28.

Marcus, S. 1985. *The Other Victorians: A Study of Sexuality and Pornography in Mid-Nineteenth Century England.* New York: W. W. Norton and Co.

Markale, J. 1975. *Celtic Civilization*. London: Gordon and Cremonesi.

Martin, F. 1951. *Nine Tales of Raven.* New York: Harper and Bros.

Meier, C. A. 1984. *The Unconscious in Its Empirical Manifestations*, E. Rolfe, trans. Boston: Sigo Press.

Mellor, A. K. 1988. *Mary Shelley: Her Life, Her Fiction, Her Monsters.* New York: Routledge, Chapman and Hall.

Neumann, E. 1963. *The Great Mother*, R. Manheim, trans. New York: Pantheon Books.

Niederland, W. G. 1984. Compulsive gambling and the "survivor syndrome." Letter. *American Journal of Psychiatry* 141(8):1013.

Ogata, S., Silk, K., Goodrich, S., Lohr, N., Westen, D., and Hills, E. 1990. Childhood sexual and physical abuse in adult patients with borderline personality disorder. *American Journal of Psychiatry* 147(8):1008–1013.

Oldham, J. M. 1989. The third individuation. In *The Middle Years*, J. M. Oldham and R. S. Liebert, eds. New Haven, Conn.: Yale University Press.

Oliver, J. E. 1988. Successive generations of child maltreatment: The children. *British Journal of Psychiatry* 153:543–553.

Otto, Walter F. 1954. *The Homeric Gods: The Spiritual Significance of Greek Religion,* Moses Hadas, trans. London: Oxford University Press.

Ovid. 1987. *Metamorphoses,* A. D. Melville, trans. New York: Pantheon.

Owens, M. E., Bill, E. L., Koester, P., and Jeppsen, E. A. 1989. Phobias and hypnotizability: A reexamination. *The International Journal of Clinical and Experimental Hypnosis* 37(3):207–216.

Peabody, J. L., and Lewis, K. 1985. Consequences of newborn intensive care. In *Infant Stress Under Intensive Care,* A. W. Gottfried and J. L. Gaiter, eds. Baltimore: University Park Press.

Pepper, Art, and Pepper, L. 1979. *Straight Life: The Story of Art Pepper.* New York: Schirmer Books.

Perrault, Charles. 1989. Little Red Riding Hood. In *Little Red Riding Hood: A Casebook,* A. Dundes, ed. Madison, Wisc.: The University of Wisconsin Press, pp. 3–6.

Pitman, R. K. 1989. Editorial: Post-traumatic stress disorder, hormones, and memory. *Biological Psychiatry* 26:221–223.

Radin, P. 1972. *The Trickster* New York: Schocken Books.

Reid, B., and Bringhurst, R. 1984. *The Raven Steals the Light.* Seattle: University of Washington Press.

Rees, A., and Rees, B. 1961. *Celtic Heritage.* London: Thames and Hudson.

Rogers, M. C. 1992. Editorial: Do the right thing—pain relief in infants and children. *New England Journal of Medicine* 326(1):55–56.

Roose, S., and Pardes, H. 1989. Biological considerations in the middle years. In *The Middle Years,* J. M. Oldham and R. S. Liebert, eds. New Haven, Conn.: Yale University Press, pp. 179–190.

Rosenheck, R. 1986. Impact of posttraumatic stress disorder of World War II on the next generation. *Journal of Nervous and Mental Disease* 174(6):319–327.

Rosenzweig, Saul. 1988. The identity and idiodynamics of multiple personality "Sally Beauchamp." *American Psychologist* 43(1):45–48.

Ross, R. J., Ball, W. A., Sullivan, K. A., and Caroff, S. N. 1989. Sleep disturbance as the hallmark of posttraumatic stress disorder. *American Journal of Psychiatry* 146(6):697–707.

Rowe, K. E. 1986. To spin a yarn: The female voice in folklore and fairy tale. In *Fairy Tales and Society*, R. Bottigheimer, ed. Philadelphia: University of Pennsylvania Press.

Shapiro, F. 1989. Efficacy of eye movement desensitization procedure in the treatment of traumatic memories. *Journal of Traumatic Stress* 2(2):199–224.

Sigurdsson, H., and Carey, S. 1988. The far reach of Tambora. *Natural History* 97(6):66–73.

Singer, A. L. 1992. *Disney's Beauty and the Beast*. New York: Disney Press.

Sjoestedt, M. L. 1982. *Gods and Heroes of the Celts*, M. Dillon, trans. Berkeley, Calif.: Turtle Island Foundation.

Sno, H. N., and Linszen, D. H. 1990. The déjà vu experience: Remembrance of things past? *American Journal of Psychiatry* 147(12):1587–1595.

Soloman, Z., Kotler, M., and Mikulincer, M. 1988. Combat related posttraumatic stress disorder among second generation Holocaust survivors: Preliminary findings. *American Journal of Psychiatry* 145(7):865–868.

Spiegel, David. 1984. Multiple personality as post–traumatic stress disorder. *Psychiatric Clinics of North America* 7(1):101–110.

_____. 1986. Dissociating damage. *American Journal of Clinical Hypnosis* 29(2):123–131.

_____. 1988. Dissociation and hypnosis in posttraumatic stress disorder. *Journal of Traumatic Stress* 1(1):17–35.

Stern, G. 1976. *Buffalo Creek Disaster*. New York: Random House.

Stevenson, Robert Louis. 1979. *The Strange Case of Dr. Jekyll and Mr. Hyde*. New York: Penguin Books.

Stone, Brian, trans. 1982. *Sir Gawain and the Green Knight*. New York: Penguin Books.

Symonds, M. 1980. The "second injury" to victims. *Evaluation and Change* (Special Issue), pp. 36–38.

Tatar, Maria. 1987. *The Hard Facts of the Grimms' Fairy Tales.* Princeton, N.J.: Princeton University Press.

Terr, L. 1979. Children of Chowchilla: A study of psychic trauma. *Psychoanalytic Study of the Child* 34:547–623.

_____. 1981. "Forbidden games": Post-traumatic child's play. *Journal of the American Academy of Child Psychiatry* 20:741–760.

_____. 1983. Time sense following psychic trauma: Clinical study of ten adults and twenty children. *American Journal of Orthopsychiatry* 53:244–261.

_____. 1987. Childhood trauma and the creative product: A look at the early lives and later works of Poe, Wharton, Magritte, Hitchcock, and Bergman. *Psychoanalytic Study of the Child* 42:545–572.

_____. 1988. Case study: What happens to the early memories of trauma? A study of twenty children under age five at the time of documented traumatic events. *Journal of the American Academy of Child Adolescent Psychiatry* 171(1):96–104.

_____. 1989a. Family anxiety after traumatic events. *Journal of Clinical Psychiatry* 50(11) (supp.):15–19.

_____. 1989b. Terror writing by the formerly terrified: A look at Stephen King. *Psychoanalytic Study of the Child* 44:36–38.

_____. 1990a. *Too Scared to Cry: Psychic Trauma in Childhood.* New York: Harper and Row.

_____. 1990b. Who's afraid in Virginia Woolf? Clues to early sexual abuse in literature. *Psychoanalytic Study of the Child* 45:533–546.

_____. 1991. Childhood traumas: An outline and overview. *American Journal of Psychiatry* 148(1):10–20.

Terry, Wallace. 1984. *Bloods: An Oral History of the Vietnam War by Black Veterans.* New York: Random House.

Titchener, J. L. 1970. Management and study of psychological response to trauma. *Journal of Trauma* 10:974–980.

Turner, Victor W. 1969. *The Ritual Process.* Chicago: Aldine Publishing Co.

Twain, Mark. 1980. *Adventures of Huckleberry Finn.* In *Mississippi Writings*, Guy Cardwell, ed. New York: The Library of America.

van der Kolk, B. 1988a. The trauma spectrum: The interaction of biological and social events in the genesis of the trauma response. *Journal of Traumatic Stress* 1(3):273–290.

_____. 1988b. The biological response to psychic trauma. In *Post–traumatic Therapy and Victims of Violence,* F. M. Ochberg, ed. New York: Brunner/Mazel, pp. 25–38.

_____. 1989. The compulsion to repeat the trauma: re–enactment, revictimization, and masochism. *Psychiatric Clinics of North America* 12(2):389–411.

van der Kolk, B., and van der Hart, O. 1989. Pierre Janet and the breakdown of adaptation in psychological trauma. *American Journal of Psychiatry* 146(12):1530–1539.

Walker, E., Katon, W., Harrap-Griffiths, J., Holm, L., Russo, J., and Hickok, L. 1988. Relationship of chronic pelvic pain to psychiatric diagnoses and childhood sexual abuse. *American Journal of Psychiatry* 145(1):75–80.

Waller, W. 1944. *The Veteran Comes Back*. New York: Drydan.

Wear, T. 1987. Nuclear denial disorder. *Journal of Humanistic Psychology* 12(3):215–219.

Wecter, D. 1944. *When Johnny Comes Marching Home*. Boston: Houghton Mifflin.

West, L. 1967. Dissociative reaction. In *The Comprehensive Textbook of Psychiatry,* A. M. Freedman and H. I. Kaplan, eds. Baltimore: Williams and Wilkins Co.

Whitmont, E. C. 1969. *The Symbolic Quest*. Princeton, N.J.: Princeton University Press.

Wilde, Oscar. 1982. *De Profundis and Other Writings.* New York: Penguin Books.

Wilson, J., and Zigelbaum, S. 1983. The Vietnam veteran on trial: The relation of post traumatic stress disorder to criminal behavior. *Behavioral Science and the Law* 1(3):69–83.

Zimmer, H. 1971. *The King and the Corpse*, J. Campbell, ed. Princeton, N.J.: Princeton University Press.

Zipes, Jack, trans. 1989. *Beauties, Beasts, and Enchantment: Classic French Fairy Tales.* New York: New American Library.

Index